UNDERSTA
The Old Tes

Derek Kidner, M.A.

Leviticus, Numbers, Deuteronomy

A BIBLE STUDY BOOK

Published in Great Britain by
Scripture Union
47 Marylebone Lane, London W1 6AX

First published 1971

Published in Daily Bible Commentary Vol. 1 1977
Reprinted 1977
First published in this edition 1978

ISBN 0 85421 632 4

Printed and bound in Great Britain by
McCorquodale (Newton) Ltd, Newton-le-Willows

INTRODUCTION

Since their introduction, Scripture Union Bible Study Books have enjoyed wide popularity both in their original paperback and more recently as the hardback Daily Bible Commentary. The continued demand has led to their production in this new format. They are unique in that they can be used both as a daily Bible reading aid and as a complete commentary on the Old Testament.

A Daily Bible Reading Aid

Each volume is divided into sections of an appropriate length for daily use. Normally each volume provides material for one quarter's use, the exceptions being 1 Kings — Job (six months) Proverbs — Isaiah (six months) and Psalms (four months). Sections have not been dated but where it has been felt appropriate that two be read together in order to complete the book within a quarter they are marked with an asterisk.

A complete commentary of the Old Testament

Every major passage is expounded with devotional warmth, clear explanations and relevance to daily life. Most commentaries follow the rather artificial verse divisions, but here the writers have been commissioned to divide the material according to the best exegetical pattern. They thus follow natural units which allow the comments to follow more closely the flow of the original writers thought.

Writers have generally based their comments on the R.S.V. and readers will probably find this is the most suitable translation to use, although the comments will be found equally helpful with any other version.

Leviticus, Numbers and Deuteronomy

INTRODUCTION

The scene of Leviticus and of Numbers **1—10** is Mount Sinai, and the content of these opening chapters is as daunting as their setting. Yet their unremitting thoroughness gives its own witness to the complete seriousness with which God takes His covenant with His people: it is no casual or arm's-length relationship, but one which must shape and colour every inch and minute of life, to train up a people whose forms of worship, structures of society and minutest details of behaviour will reflect the holiness of God. Without these chapters we should have had little if any idea of the many facets of sacrifice to which the N.T. makes reference; the high and fearful demands of priesthood; the meaning of the rent veil of the Temple and the bearing away of sin which the great Day of Atonement expounded in advance; nor should we have heard the second of the great commandments, '. . . love your neighbour as yourself', nor understood the meaning of Jubilee and of Nazirites, nor pictured the array of Israel's camp and the order of their march.

By way of contrast, the remainder of Numbers (**11—36**) tells the absorbing story of reluctant, mutinous pilgrims and the eventual arrival of their children at the threshold of the Promised Land after a series of stresses, altercations and seductions which the N.T. treats as standing examples and warnings to the Church (1 Cor. **10**.1–13; Heb. **3**; Jude 5,11; Rev. **2**.14). Interspersed with these events are various laws, ecclesiastical (e.g. tithes, ritual cleansing, festal sacrifices) and civil (e.g. vows, inheritance, homicide), and the log of Israel's travels (**33**).

Deuteronomy tells of Moses' last, solemn charge to Israel. It has a warmth and eloquence all its own, and (as various recent scholars have pointed out) its pattern strikingly reflects the structure of a treaty covenant, with its preamble, historical survey, basic principles, detailed stipulations, confirmatory blessings and cursings, witnesses, and the injunction that copies of the covenant must be preserved and periodically read in public. For details, see the commentary. To make this preaching of the Law indelible, its challenge is summed up in the Song of Moses (**32**), and then the Pentateuch is brought to a fitting end by the oracle giving the destinies of the twelve tribes, and by the restrained but moving account of Moses' death.

Leviticus

OUTLINE

1. THE FIVE STANDARD SACRIFICES: chs. 1—7

A. BASIC REGULATIONS: 1.1—6.7

1 The Burnt Offering
2 The Cereal Offering
3 The Peace Offering
4.1—5.13 The Sin Offering
5.14—6.7 The Guilt Offering

B. PRIESTLY REGULATIONS: 6.8—7.38

6.8—7.38 Procedures for the Five Offering

2. THE PRIESTHOOD INAUGURATED. chs. 8—10

8, 9 The Priesting
10 The Priesthood Marred

3. THE CLEAN AND THE UNCLEAN: chs. 11—15

11 'Taste not, Touch not'
12 Defilement by Childbirth
13 Defilement by 'Leprosy'
14 The Cleansing of 'Leprosy'
15 Defilement by a Discharge

4. THE DAY OF ATONEMENT: ch. 16

5. A HOLY NATION: chs. 17—27

17 Precious Blood
18 Sexual Sanity
19, 20 Unclassified Ordinances
21 Priestly Purity
22 More about Priests and Offerings
23 The Sacred Calendar
24 Unbroken Homage
25 Sabbatical Year and Jubilee
26 A Concluding Charge to Israel
27 An Appendix on Valuations

1. THE FIVE STANDARD SACRIFICES: Leviticus 1—7
A. BASIC REGULATIONS: 1.1—6.7

Leviticus 1 — The Burnt Offering

The broad regulations of this chapter are supplemented by further details in **6**.8–13. But first note the setting, a characteristic O.T. blend of grace and judgement. Israel, liberated and brought into covenant, is encamped at Sinai, and the glory of the Lord has sealed the great enterprise of erecting the 'tent of meeting' (1; cf. Exod. **40**.34) where God will have fellowship with man. Yet this very glory has kept Moses at a distance (Exod. **40**.35), and Leviticus will constantly bear witness to God's overwhelming holiness.

By its name (lit., 'that which ascends') and by its ritual the burnt offering showed its Godward emphasis. It was the only sacrifice, among the five types in chs. **1—5**, which provided no food for either priest or worshipper. So the crown rights of God and the joy of giving *away* were established at the outset, while the gradation of values, from a bull down to a pair of pigeons, allowed everyone the opportunity to bring some gift. Each was of equal fragrance (9,13,17), when offered from the heart (Psa. **51**.17, 19); each on any other terms was an affront (Psa. **51**.16; **50**.9 ff.).

Yet sacrifice was harsh and violent, and the offerer was to know it, his own hand pressed on the creature's head (4; see comment on **3**.2), his own act doing it to death. And his part in the proceedings, while it emphasized his personal responsibility, could not be construed as achieving his acceptance. True, the victim was his gift, but its atoning value (4) was *God's* gift (see **17**.11), while his own role was mere butchery (5,6: to kill, flay and cut up). It was the priest's part to give it the form of a sacrifice, bringing it to God. The bulk of the chapter is about this.

The O.T. knew the inadequacy of such victims (e.g. Psa. **40**.6–8) and of such priests (e.g. Lev. **4**.3). The N.T. finds in Christ the one real priest and sacrifice (e.g. Heb. **9**.6 f., 11 f.), who 'gave Himself up for us, a fragrant offering' (Eph. **5**.2; cf. Lev. **1**.9,13,17). Sanctified by Him (Heb. **10**.14), the Christian can become a living sacrifice himself (Rom. **12**.1), called to offer the worship and praise (1 Pet. **2**.5; Heb. **13**.15 f.) which are not drama but reality.

Concerning this offering see also **6**.14–23; Num. **15**.1–10. The word 'cereal' is a translator's convenience; the Hebrew simply calls it an 'offering', using a word which implies a token of homage. In these laws it is a technical term for offerings that involved no shedding of blood, so the translation is a fair one; but in Gen. **4**.3–5 it is used equally of Cain's gift and Abel's, and there are other such passages. In civil life it stood for tribute or a formal gift: cf. Gen. **33**.10; 2 Kings **17**.3 f.; Psa. **45**.12.

Offered to God, it was not only homage but the acknowledgement and dedication of His staple gifts. It made no atonement since it cost no life (cf. Heb. **9**.22); but it was to accompany the blood-shedding sacrifices, as Num. **15**.1–10 indicates. God was presented again with His own gifts, yet not in their natural state (there was a place for this: cf. v. 12; **23**.10, etc.) but in the forms given them in human use: fine flour, not grain; oil, not olives; and so on. The domesticity of vs. 4–7, with their recipes and utensils (a griddle [5] was a metal baking-plate), reinforces the point, setting aside ordinary things, at their best, for God in token (the 'memorial portion') and for His ministers in actuality; using the unspoken language of hospitality, of the kind that Abraham and Sarah gave in Gen. **18**.6 ff. when they entertained angels unawares. So Acts **10**.4 describes the practical piety of Cornelius in terms of this offering (cf. vs. 2,9,16).

But there are no concessions to familiarity. Every feature of the memorial portion emphasized its holiness: its consecration by anointing (1; see on **8**.10 ff.); its frankincense used up for God (2; cf. Psa. **141**.2); its ascent in fire (2). The ban on honey and leaven (11) strikes the same note, for it only applied to fire-offerings, as v. 12 makes clear. These substances were among the minor luxuries of life, matters for gratitude (12; cf. **7**.13), but more eloquent of God's bounty than of His demands (cf. Exod. **12**.39; **13**.7–9; Prov. **25**.16).

Note, finally, 'the salt of the covenant' (13), a reminder of the table fellowship that had confirmed the bond between God and His people (Exod. **24**.8–11). In this way every sacrifice was to contain an allusion to this host-and-guest relationship (see Ezra **4**.14; cf. 'a covenant of salt', Num. **18**.19; 2 Chron. **13**.5). Such is God's fidelity; such, too, He expects from us (13) and, it would seem from Mark **9**.50b, between us.

Leviticus 3 — The Peace Offering

Nothing in this chapter gives any hint of what would have loomed largest in a human account: that this offering was festive, a meal as well as a sacrifice. This aspect will emerge in **7**.11–36 (cf. **17**.1–7, and the further law of Deut. **12**.20–28), but the present concern is with more primary matters: the fitness of the victim (1,6), its slaughter by and for the worshipper (2a,8a,13a; see further, next paragraph), its blood hurled against the altar (2b,8b,13b), and the burning of what belonged exclusively to God (3–5,9–11,14–16). Without these the meal would have been mere camaraderie or a pleasant fellowship meal; with them its fellowship could be fundamentally 'with the Father', as the N.T. would put it, and thereby genuinely 'with one another' (see 1 John **1**.3,7).

The symbolism of laying one's hand on the victim's head (2, etc.) was that of substitution. The action largely spoke for itself, but any ambiguity is removed in Num. **8**.10–19, where see comment.

The law against eating fat (16b,17) is elaborated a little in **7**.22–25. There is, incidentally, no conflict with this rule in Neh. **8**.10, where a different word is used. Whether the fat was devoted to God as being the richest part (as Gen. **4**.4 seems to imply) or, like the blood, as symbolizing life, we are not told; the food laws seldom offer their reasons. But by marking out (for a while—cf. Col. **2**.16 f.) certain areas of life as God's preserves and not man's, the levitical laws gave a continual reminder of both sovereignty and grace. Sovereignty, in that it is for God to choose what He will give or withhold; grace, in that what He withholds He turns to our benefit. The blood (17) was 'given' back for better use than nourishment (**17**.11). The fat, 'as food offered by fire to the Lord' (11), was made the symbol of the fact that we do not feast alone, but play host to God Himself, by His gracious command. He dines with us, as well as we with Him.

Leviticus 4 — The Sin Offering

With regard to the sin offering, see also **6**.24–30. The scope of this sacrifice is defined by the word 'unwittingly', repeated in each paragraph (2,13,22,27). I.e. it was not the offering *par excellence* for a man convicted of his general sinfulness, for the Law could provide no single 'full, perfect and sufficient sacrifice'; rather, it met the kind of need indicated by Psa. **19**.12 as distinct from 13. Cf. Num. **15**.22–31. It could almost be called the Lapse Offering; for 'unwittingly' translates a word which implies not so much ignorance as stumbling or straying.

The degree to which different classes of offender affected others by their sin seems to be reflected in the descending scale of victims. The 'anointed priest' (3), whose sin involved the whole people, was probably the high priest, anointed more liberally than his fellows (cf. **8**.12 with v. 30; Psa. **133**.2). Verse 3 reveals the impossible burden of priesthood; Heb. **7**.27 f. names the only bearer of it equal to the task. But some such responsibility is inseparable from all leadership (cf. Jas. **3**.1; Heb. **13**.17).

Notice the strong emphasis on the blood, recovering the sinner's lost access to God. For his own offence (3–12) or the congregation's (13–21), the high priest could no longer minister in the sanctuary until blood had made atonement at the places where he would stand before God: the veil, the incense altar and, in the courtyard, the altar of burnt offering. The sevenfold sprinkling (6,17), the daubing of the incense altar's horns, and the pouring of the remaining blood round the main altar (7,18), formed a more elaborate sequence than the single rapid movement of throwing the blood against the altar, prescribed for the offerings of chs. **1** and **3**. The modified ritual for the individual, whether ruler (22–26) or private citizen (27–35), made the same point by being enacted at *his* customary meeting place with God, the main altar (25,30,34). See further, on **10**.12–20.

Amid these complexities, note the implied seriousness of the sins we might think excusable; but also the simple assurance of the refrain, 'the priest shall make atonement for him . . ., and he shall be forgiven' (20 [plural], 26,31,35). Study, finally, the challenging parable that Heb. **13**.11–14 finds in the instructions of vs. 12 and 21. 'Let us go forth to Him . . .'.

Leviticus 5.1—6.7 — Sin Offering and Guilt Offering

The Sin Offering (continued, **5**.1–13). There is little doubt that these verses round off the regulations of ch. **4**, still speaking of the sin offering rather than the guilt offering (see **5**.14—**6**.7). Although **5**.6a,7a suggest the latter, they are subject to vs. 6b,7b, which are supported by vs. 8,9,11,12 in speaking of the sin offering. (Note that in **4**.13,22,27 the actions that demand a sin offering make the offender 'guilty', as do those of **5**.2–5; it is a somewhat similar linking of terms in vs. 6a,7a here.)

The pattern of **5**.1–13 is simple: first, some examples of offences that called for this sacrifice (1–4)—minor liberties taken with God's majesty and holiness; and secondly, the sacrifice itself (5–13), with the concessions to various degrees of poverty. It is probably vs.

11–13 that account for the word 'almost' in Heb. **9**.22; an exception that proves the absence of magical views of the inherent power of blood.

The Guilt Offering (**5**.14—**6**.7). For this, the distinctive notes are the costing of the sacrifice ('valued by you . . .', **5**.15,18; **6**.6; cf. 1 Pet. **1**.18 f.) and the more-than-full repayment of the damage (**5**.16, etc.). It portrays the element of 'satisfaction' in atonement, and of restitution in repentance; it is this term that describes the sacrifice of the Servant in Isa. **53**.10.

The first case here (**5**.14–16) refers to what Mal. **3**.6 ff. calls 'robbing' God: i.e. using for oneself the tithes, firstfruits, etc., which are God's due and therefore 'holy'; hence the monetary repayment in v. 16. The second case (**5**.17–19) seems to correspond to Psa. **19**.12, Jer. **17**.9, etc., in that some guilt is known only to God, and there can be atonement but not restitution. The third group of cases (**6**.1–7), which incidentally draws out some of the implications of 'Thou shalt not steal', makes classically clear the Biblical principle that no sin is purely a man-to-man affair. This emerges not only from the fact that manward restitution is not enough (the transaction of vs. 4,5 must be followed by the atoning sacrifice of vs. 6,7), but from the significant phrasing of v. 2a. The whole paragraph is an anticipation of our Lord's dictum, 'first be reconciled to your brother' (Matt. **5**.23 f.).

B. PRIESTLY REGULATIONS: **6**.8—**7**.38

Leviticus 6.8—7.10 — Procedures for Four Offerings

Specialized though these directives are, they supply further insights into the rituals already prescribed in chs. **1—5**.

The Burnt Offering (**6**.8–13). Thoroughness and preparedness are demanded by the law of the altar fire: the sacrifice wholly consumed (9) and the fire always burning (12 f.). The vigilance that this required of the priests was matched by that of the singers (1 Chron. **9**.33; Psa. **134**.1 f.), and the beautiful figure of Psa. **5**.3 is clearly derived from v. 12. It is no far cry to the call of Luke **12**.35–40 or of Rom. **12**.11. Regarding the quarantine-like precautions of **6**.10 f., they will only seem excessive if one takes a popular estimate of holiness and sin, which they are designed to correct. The lesson was as unwelcome to ancient Israel as to modern man: see Ezek. **44**.6–8,15–19.

The Cereal Offering (**6**.14–23). Note the phrase, 'their portion of My offerings' (17). Part of the concern of vs. 14–18 is to teach a true attitude to 'giving and receiving' (Phil. **4**.15). The giver is shown that he makes an offering to God, not a dole to a dependant; and the receiver, that his share is by rights a gift from heaven, not simply the 'perks' of the job. Paul may have had this passage in mind when he developed the theme in sacrificial terms in Phil. **4**.18.

The Sin Offering and Guilt Offering (**6**.24—**7**.7). The rituals for these were very similar, as **7**.7 points out. The reason for the rule against eating the sin offering in the circumstances of **6**.30 was doubtless that the priest was personally implicated in both cases where this ritual was prescribed: on his own account (**4**.3,6) or as a member of 'the whole congregation' (**4**.13,17). The distinction between his capacity as mediator and as worshipper is seen too in the different rules for the cereal offering (vs. 18,23).

The portion for the priest (**7**.8–10). After v. 7 it is convenient to list the portions allotted to the sacrificing priest on other occasions. The fact that these are God's bounty from offerings due to Him (see on **6**.17) is not mentioned here: the recipients are given the security of a fixed share, as of right. The N.T. uses the matter-of-fact term 'wages' (Luke **10**.7; 1 Tim. **5**.18) in this kind of context. God may test His servants by shortage, but He does not show a preference for pauperizing them.

Leviticus 7.11–38 Procedure for the Peace Offering

The instructions in ch. 3 made no mention of the meal that followed the sacrifice, nor of the priest's allotted share; the whole concern was with making an acceptable offering to God. Now the secondary matters can follow.

Thanks, vows and freewill gifts (11–18). Notice the inclusion of leavened bread alongside unleavened (12 f.); see the comment on **2**.11 ff. As for the requirement that the meat must be eaten the same day (15) or, in the case of vows and freewill gifts, within two days (16–18), its main purpose may have been to ensure that the feast was shared, and shared widely. The large company glimpsed in e.g. Deut. **12**.18 f. would be almost a necessity for this, especially in the thanksgiving feast, whereas the celebration of a vow that had been heard, or of a gift that one was moved to offer, could be kept within a smaller circle if one desired it. While the risk to health could well account for the rule against keeping the meat for a third day (17 f.), the variation between one and two days points to another kind of concern, such as the one we have suggested.

How and what one might eat (19–27). The lesson conveyed by the distinction between clean and unclean (19–21) is touched on in the comment on **6**.10 f., and the significance of the ban on fat and blood is discussed at **3**.16b f. The phrase 'cut off from his people' (20, etc.)

first occurs in Gen. **17**.14, where the uncircumcised suffers this penalty because he has 'broken My covenant'. I.e., it is excommunication, not for inadvertence (which was quickly remedied: cf., e.g. **11**.24–28), but for arrogance. It is not said to be irreversible.

Wave offering and heave offering (28–36). The second of these terms should possibly be translated simply 'offering' (RSV) or 'contribution', i.e. something 'removed' from the main mass rather than 'lifted up' before God. But the latter gesture would have effectively conveyed the fact that the priest's share was first of all the Lord's, and 'heave offering' may well be the right translation. The 'wave offering' (30,34) was probably waved not from side to side but towards the altar and back (the verb is used of the movement of a saw in Isa. **10**.15), perhaps to indicate offering it and receiving it back from the Lord, in a gesture as simple in its symbolism as that of the 'heave offering'.

Questions for further study and discussion on Leviticus chs. 1—7

1. Leviticus (like Exodus and Numbers) literally begins with the word 'And'. Follow up this clue to its place in the total pattern of the Pentateuch.
2. How are we to regard these sacrifices? As the outsider's way back to God, or as the insider's pattern of worship?
3. Do you find any significance in the order in which the sacrifices are dealt with in these chapters?
4. Choose a N.T. reading to go with each of the five sacrifices.

2. THE PRIESTHOOD INAUGURATED: Leviticus 8—10

Leviticus 8 — The First Stage of Priesting

At long last the instructions recorded in Exod. **29**; **30**.22–30; **40**.9–15 are due to be completed. The ceremony links together the high priest, his fellow priests and the place where they minister, in rituals differing with their various functions but united by the common feature of anointing or sprinkling with oil (vs. 10–12,30), which signified God's ownership (10c,11c,12c; cf. Gen. **28**.17 f.) or, in the case of men, His commission (e.g. 1 Kings **19**.16) and the endowment of the Spirit for particular tasks (e.g. Isa. **61**.1; 1 John **2**.27). The richness of oil also gave it the pleasant connotation of festivity (cf. Isa. **61**.3; Psa. **45**.7; **104**.15), and its pervasiveness made it an apt symbol of unity, as it spread its fragrance over the diversity of the high-priestly robes (cf. v. 12 with Psa. **133**). This diversity included the names of the twelve tribes of Israel, engraved on the stones set in ephod and breastpiece (cf. vs. 7 f. with Exod.

28.9–12,17–21,29). Against such a background of anointed priests, prophets and kings must be seen the title of the Lord's anointed, the Messiah or Christ.

The Urim and Thummim (8) were apparently used for ascertaining God's Yes or No by drawing lots. Possibly these lots were matching stones, showing the answer according to whichever surface was uniformly uppermost when they were withdrawn from the breast-piece (cf. 1 Sam. **14**.37,41 f., RSV)—while a lack of uniformity indicated no answer. But this is conjecture; what is clear is that God's answer was given or withheld at His own will. The contrast between this form of enquiry and those of divination and necromancy (where man attempts to pierce God's secrets) is firmly drawn: cf. Num. **23**.23; 1 Sam. **28**.6,7 ff.; Isa. **44**.24–26.

The word 'ordination' ('consecration', AV [KJV], RV) in vs. 22, 28, etc., is from a Hebrew root connected with fullness. It is used of the 'setting' which a jewel fills (Exod. **28**.17), and could possibly emphasize the 'installing' of the priests in office. But it is coupled with the term (lit.) 'fill your hand' (RSV 'ordain you') in v. 33c, which evidently refers to the symbolism of v. 27 whereby the priest was entrusted for the first time with the offerings which would be his lifelong concern.

The applying of blood to the right ear, etc., in vs. 23 f. signified its application to the whole body, since these were the extremities and the right side was valued above the left (cf., e.g. Gen. **48**.13 ff.). Probably we should not read into it the further O.T. associations of, e.g. the ear with obedience (Isa. **50**.5), etc., which obscure the real point here, the claiming of the man in his entirety, a living sacrifice for God.

Leviticus 9 — The Priesting Completed

'The eighth day' (1) recalls the words 'It will take seven days to ordain you' (**8**.33), days of waiting at the threshold (**8**.35) as neither priests nor laymen (Moses was their priest throughout ch. **8**). But by itself the vigil, though it emphasized the thorough preparation, still brought them no admission: only the blood of atonement could do this.

Following almost the whole gamut of offerings in vs. 2–4, there is the promise of glory (6), true to the sequence regularly found in the N.T. (e.g. Luke **24**.26; Rom. **8**.18 ff.; Heb. **2**.9 f.); but here the mediator was the first to need atonement, and the suffering was not his own. RSV's 'Then' in v. 15 is useful in highlighting the prelimin-aries that had to take place before an imperfect high priest could save his people. Heb. **7**.26 ff. makes the point and draws a contrast.

The blessing of the people (22) was no empty gesture but an effective transmission of God's power; an example of its meaning is shown in Deut. **28**.1–14. It was the special calling of the priests 'to bless in the name of the Lord' (Deut. **21**.5), and the priestly gesture of v. 22 was to be our Lord's parting one (Luke **24**.50 f.) after His fulfilment of 'the sin offering and the burnt offering and the peace offerings' (22).

Notice, finally, the tokens of God's presence (23 f.), majestic even in grace. The people's exultant and awestruck response shows two ingredients of worship, in primitive vigour—not softened by familiarity. To record a more modern reaction to God's presence, v. 24 might have had to read, 'they dragged themselves to their feet, and mumbled'.

Leviticus 10 — The Priesthood Marred

Significantly, the priests are no sooner ordained than in trouble. Their special temptation is to presume on their position, and improve on their instructions. Cf. the pressure on our Lord to force the pace (Matt. **4**.6 f.); cf. the carnal deviations which Paul had to rebuke in the young churches (e.g. Gal. **1**.6; Col. **2**.8 ff.). The Church does not always take kindly to being under the word of God.

The fire and glory of vs. 2 f. throw back a fierce light on the episode of **9**.23 f., where it was the sacrifice that was consumed, not the offerer. They are also visible reminders of the judgement which even God's saving presence precipitates: cf. John **3**.17 ff.; Heb. **10**.26–31; **12**.25–28. Such is holiness, and the truth about it was the answer Aaron needed and accepted (3). David was to learn a similar lesson through Uzzah's fate (2 Sam. **6**.8–15), and Isaiah through Uzziah's (2 Chron. **26**.16,21; Isa. **6**.1 ff.).

The remainder of the chapter draws out some detailed implications of v. 3. (Further issues, which are quite crucial, emerge in ch. **16**.)

No respite from responsibility (4–7). To be unkempt (6a), in surrender to private grief, would be to become ritually unclean. Continuing to stand between God and man, as they must (7), they would then transmit wrath instead of blessing (6b). Cf. Samuel's sense of inescapable responsibility, in a different context: 1 Sam. **12**.23.

No strong drink on duty (8–11). How directly this injunction bore on Nadab and Abihu's offence, we simply are not told. But their fate underlined the danger of careless handling of what was holy. Verse 11, however, goes beyond physical to mental fitness for the priest's hardest and most neglected task: cf. Deut. **33**.10a; Hos. **4**.6–11; Mal. **2**.7 f.

The priest completes the sacrifice (12–15; 16–20). Once more the priest as mediator is distinguished from the priest as individual. As the latter, he was entitled to the parts of certain offerings as his emoluments (14 f.); but as the former, he played a vital part in the ritual of an offering's acceptance (12 f., 17,19b). The climax of some sacrifices was their ascent in smoke; of others it was the bringing of their blood inside the holy place (**4**.6 f., 17 f.) or the holy of holies (**16**.14 f.); while of others it was their consumption by the priest in the sanctuary (v. 18 agrees with ch. **4** that the last of these applied when the second did not). In this last case, priest and victim together were to 'take away' iniquity (17b, RV marg.) and make atonement (17b)—not by the priest's eating a sin-laden carcase, for it was 'most holy' (**6**.25), but by his completion of the bringing of the slain victim before God. This identification of priest and sacrifice made all too little sense when Aaron (19b) or any son of his was the mediator. The discord would only resolve itself in Christ (Heb. **9**.23–28).

3. THE CLEAN AND THE UNCLEAN: Leviticus 11—15

Leviticus 11 — 'Taste not, Touch not'

Food laws (**11**.1–23,41–47). Several of the names, especially of the birds, are of uncertain meaning to us; and the generalizations about certain classes (e.g. vs. 3,9 f., 20) offer no reason for the rules that apply to them, only a simple guide to their use (e.g. 'chews the cud', in vs. 5,6, is a convenient, not a technical, description). Different principles may have governed different examples, cultic in some cases, hygienic or aesthetic in others; what mattered for the Israelite was that God had drawn these distinctions and made them an object-lesson in practical holiness.

The old view that the pig (7) was banned chiefly as a danger to health, rather than as an animal prominent in heathen rites, is vigorously defended by W. F. Albright (*Yahweh and the Gods of Canaan*, 1968), who points out that the creatures of vs. 5 and 6 are also disease-carriers, not cultic animals. (Possibly the camel [4] was prohibited in order to keep the classification of v. 3 uncomplicated by exceptions). Albright also notes the distinction between free-swimming and mud-burrowing aquatic creatures (9–12), which broadly corresponds to their possession or lack of fins and scales, and has special relevance to the transmission of disease in places where water is slow moving.

The disqualifying element in vs. 13–19 appears to be that these are birds of prey, ritually unacceptable because of the blood they consume. In vs. 20–23, 29 f., 41 f., an aesthetic principle may enter in, to exclude creatures that are repulsive-looking as being demeaning to the eater; but the main consideration seems to be their close contact with the earth (contrast v. 21 with 41–43), which calls to mind the curse on the serpent in Gen. **3**.14.

With regard to these regulations in general, notice the opportunity they were to provide in Isa. **66**.17 of offering studied insults to God. This is one extreme; the other is Pharisaism; the gospel delivers us from both (cf. Rom. **7**.4–11; **8**.2–4; Col. **2**.16–23).

Defilement by contact (**11**.24–40). The reference of v. 26 is evidently to carcasses, as in the rest of the passage. The rules for decontamination, strict as they are, take account of practical necessities. The 'quarantine' is short (24b, etc.) and the cleansing straightforward (e.g. 28,32). This moderation, together with the distinctions made in vs. 32–38 between relatively washable and unwashable, absorbent and non-absorbent materials, and between different quantities and states of water in vs. 34,36, implies a commonsense approach which discourages Pharisaic extremes at the same time that it reiterates the central lesson, 'Be holy, for I am holy' (44 f.; cf. 1 Pet. **1**.16).

Leviticus 12 — Defilement by Childbirth

This unpromising chapter was to give rise to the first two events recorded of our Lord after His birth, and set the scene for the prophecies of Simeon and Anna: Luke **2**.21–39. It not only prepared the conditions in which His birth 'under the law' (Gal. **4**.4) would be made plain from the start (cf. Luke **2**.22,27,39), but provided our only secure clue to His initial poverty (8, cf. Luke **2**.24).

The terms 'unclean' and 'clean' which dominate this group of chapters are ceremonial, not moral; cf. the expression 'their purification' in Luke **2**.22 (RV, RSV), which refers to the infant Christ's involvement in His mother's uncleanness by the law of v. 2b (its provisions are set out in Lev. **15**.19 ff.). A child's sinfulness from its conception onwards (Psa. **51**.5) is not in view here; see further on vs. 6–8. But while Scripture regards marriage and procreation as God's good gifts (e.g. Psa. **127**.3; Heb. **13**.4), it also makes this area the first to come under judgement at the Fall. There may be an intended reminder of Gen. **3**.16 in this law; possibly, too, of the promise of Gen. **3**.15 in the shortened period of uncleanness for the birth of a boy (2–4,5). The boy's circumcision, however (3), may have counted towards the cleansing, as some have suggested.

The two stages of ritual uncleanness (the week or fortnight and the additional 33 or 66 days) were at two levels of stringency: in the first period the mother's uncleanness was, so to speak, contagious

(2b,5a, cf. **15**.19 ff.), while in the second it only debarred her from holy things and places (4).

In the purifying rite (6–8), the burnt offering, with its emphasis on dedication, preceded the sin offering. This unusual order (in contrast to, e.g. **8**.14,18; **9**.7; **14**.19) tends to confirm that the thought of personal sin was not prominent here; the cleansing was 'from the flow of her blood' (7), not from any guilt attached to marital intercourse or childbirth. Notice, finally, that the element of dedication, implicit in the burnt offering, was uppermost in Luke **2**.22, where the occasion was used as the opportunity to give back Mary's firstborn to the Lord.

Leviticus 13 — Defilement by 'Leprosy'

According to a leading authority on leprosy, Dr. R. G. Cochrane, 'the modern disease of leprosy bears no resemblance to that described in the Bible' (*Biblical Leprosy*, Tyndale Press, 1961), and this view is endorsed by various O.T. scholars. The same Hebrew term applies to certain mildews and fungi in materials (**13**.47–59; **14**.33–53) as to the several kinds of sores and infections described here, whose symptoms (and, above all, curability) distinguish them from the leprosy we know. For suggested identifications, see the commentaries.

The priest's careful procedure, with its provision for a three-stage examination where necessary (e.g. vs. 4–6), is an impressive diagnostic exercise. But ritual defilement rather than physical contagion was the point at issue, though the two would coincide in many cases. The chief signs of a defiling malady were, variously: depth, local bleaching of the hair (3,20, etc.), active spread (7,22, etc.) and rawness (10,14, etc.). In connection with the last of these, note vs. 9–17 which show why such lepers as Gehazi, 'as white as snow', were not automatically isolated (2 Kings **5**.1,27; **8**.4 f., cf. perhaps Num. **12**.10–15). This condition, perhaps leukoderma, was repulsive, as Aaron's appalling description of Miriam makes all too plain (Num. **12**.12), but only called for isolation if open sores broke out (Lev. **13**.14–17). The whiteness, incidentally, confirms that what we call leprosy is a different disease, since 'the lesions of leprosy are never white' (R. G. Cochrane, ibid.).

The torn clothes, etc., of v. 45 were signs of mourning (cf. **10**.6; Ezek. **24**.17), as though the banished man were mourning his own death; yet the words 'as long as he has the disease' (46) hold out some hope, which the next chapter will reinforce. The intense signs of grief and shame put this ceremonial defilement in a class by itself, and support the view that it was intended to illustrate the havoc of sin. This impression is strengthened by the fact that leprosy was inflicted as a judgement on at least three people in the O.T. (Miriam, Gehazi and Uzziah) and by the allusion to the leper's cleansing which is made in the penitential Psa. **51**.7 (cf. Lev. **14**.6 f.). If the passage on mildew in a garment (47–59) is in mind in Jude 23, it provides another indication of the moral symbolism of this chapter.

Leviticus 14 — The Cleansing of 'Leprosy'

(*i*) *In a human sufferer* (1–32). The procedure, summarized, was first the patient's examination and clearance (the ritual must be based on truth), then the first purification rites and partial restoration (4–9), finally, on the eighth day, the sacrifices for atonement (10–20, 21–32).

The hyssop (4), a bushy plant, was evidently to be bound to the cedar stick with the scarlet material, to make a mop for the sprinkling mentioned in v. 7. Its somewhat similar use at the first Passover (Exod. **12**.22) gave it an obvious appropriateness, as did the cedar's resistance to decay and the scarlet stuff's blood-red appearance. All three were also used in preparing the cleansing water described in Num. **19.6**.

The 'running water' (5) was understood in later Judaism to mean water taken from a spring (implying its purity) but held in the bowl which received the blood. It would be hard to imagine a more vivid symbolism of death, cleansing and liberation (on the last of these see below, on v. 53) in all of which the healed man was made a participant by the sevenfold sprinkling (7; cf. 1 Pet. **1**.2). Note the purifying by water and blood, and the explicit pronouncement (7b) which resolved any ambiguity which the actions might have had concerning the crucial question—for sacraments without words establish nothing.

The subsequent atoning rites (10–20 or 21–32) are remarkable for prescribing the whole range of sacrifices except the peace offering (which no doubt was often voluntarily added for a thanksgiving celebration), and for treating the reclaimed man almost as if he were a priest, earmarked for God with blood and oil (14,17, cf. **8**.23,30). [*Note:* The 'log' of oil (10) was about $\frac{1}{3}$ litre.] It was a characteristic divine gesture of grace superabounding where, in picture, sin had abounded.

(*ii*) *In a house* (33–53). With this, compare the 'leprosy' in a garment, **13**.47–59. As with the food laws, these regulations make good sense physically, but were primarily a means of sharpening the Israelite's sense of what is clean or unclean before God. This is clear from the ritual regulations of vs. 46 f. (inadequate as health rules) and especially those of vs. 48 ff., closely akin to the means of purifying the human leper. Incidentally the release of the living bird (53) in connection with cleansing a house suggests that it symbolizes a removal of uncleanness (cf. the scapegoat, **16**.22) rather than a resurrection, both here and in v. 7. In all these areas it is made very clear that the bold symbolism of the ritual was to be the counterpart of practical action that was equally bold, realistic and ruthless in excluding every sign of corruption.

Leviticus 15 — Defilement by a Discharge

The subject is of discharges from the genital organs, and the pattern of the chapter is symmetrical, dealing first with pathological (1–15) and normal (16–18) cases in males, and then with normal (19–24) and pathological (25–30) cases in females, before leading on to a statement of the law's purpose (31) and the summary (32 f.).

The isolating effect of an abnormal discharge was second only to that of leprosy, cutting off the person concerned not only from the sanctuary (31) but from almost any share in social life. The restrictions of, e.g. vs. 4–12 amounted to a perpetual quarantine, whereas those of vs. 16–18 involved no one else and were quickly over. In the case of women, the regulations for normal and abnormal states differed only in duration and in requiring sacrifices for the latter group (29 f., cf. 14 f. for males). On v. 24 see comment on ch. **18**.19.

So the chapter illuminates the plight of the woman afflicted for twelve years with an issue of blood, and her 'fear and trembling' (Mark **5**.33) at the discovery of her contact with the crowd and with Jesus. Her case shows up the limitations of the Law, which could isolate uncleanness (31) but could not cure it (cf. Gal. **3**.21 f.).

What is left unsaid here is that the commonest cause of persistent discharges is gonorrhoea, a disease of promiscuity. While some who suffered under this law would be innocent (and were not accused by it), others would know that they had themselves to blame, and would find the analogy between ceremonial and moral defilement uncomfortably close.

Verse 31 is an important statement of the principle involved in this group of laws, soon to be rigorously enforced in Num. **5**.1–4. In the Exodus period the searching implications of God's presence were shown by immediate interventions (cf. **9**.24; **10**.2). At other times the warning, 'lest they die', was implemented by more gradual or inward processes (e.g. Ezek. **18**.31; **24**.21–23; John **8**.24; **15**.22), but never withdrawn. Access to this perfect holiness is for 'hearts sprinkled clean' and 'bodies washed with pure water' (Heb. **10**.22). The positive side of this is indicated by the unusual verb for 'keep . . .

separate', which is the root of the word Nazirite—a reminder of Israel's high calling, a people consecrated to special service.

Questions for further study and discussion on Leviticus chs. 8—15

1. What aspects of the priesthood of Christ are illustrated by the garments, the ordination rites and the duties of Aaron and his sons?
2. In what sense does the N.T. show that earthly priests are obsolete (see Heb. **5—10**), and in what sense is the Church 'a holy priesthood' (see 1 Pet. **2**.5; Heb. **13**.10–16)?
3. Study the relation of Col. **2**.16 f. and Mark **7**.18 f. to the laws on the clean and the unclean in, e.g. Lev. **11**. What did Christ abolish in Mark 7.1–23, and what did He retain?
4. In the light of Question 3, do you think it a fair summary to say that the Christian is bound by the moral laws of the O.T., but not by its ceremonial and civil regulations? If so, what is the present value of the latter two? What other N.T. passages throw light on this?

4. THE DAY OF ATONEMENT

Leviticus 16 — The Way into the Holiest

This chapter is one of the most important in the Law, and looms large in the Epistle to the Hebrews. It was given urgency by its tragic context (1).

The fact that the high priest's own access to the Holy of Holies had to be won by sacrifice (11–14) before he could re-enter on his people's behalf (15 ff.), was proof enough of the priesthood's inadequacy (cf. Heb. **5**.3; **7**.27; **9**.7). The cloud of incense, to hide God's throne from Aaron 'lest he die' (13), re-emphasized the lesson; in fact the whole chapter calls attention to man's distance from God by the very thoroughness of its procedure, from the opening warning, 'not to come at all times' (2), to the closing emphasis on the ubiquitous defilement of sin (33).

Verses 6–10 use the common O.T. technique of presenting an outline account before coming to the fuller details, which follow in vs. 11–22. The word Azazel (8,10,26) need not be a name; it should be understood in the light of vs. 20–22, which would support the meaning 'dismissal' (RV marg.) or 'entire removal' (BDB Lexicon, p. 736). In later Judaism, Azazel is the name of a demon, but this could have originated from a misunderstanding of this very passage. The Septuagint, the earliest Jewish translation, has simply 'dismissal'. Just as the first ceremony (11–14,15–19) is the classic illustration of atonement as opening the way *in* ('within', vs. 2,12,15; cf. Heb. **9**.12; **10**.19–22), so the scapegoat ritual exemplifies supremely the concept of having sin laid 'upon' the victim (22; cf. Isa. **53**.4–6; 1 Pet. **2**.24) and taken 'away' (21; cf. Psa. **103**.12; John **1**.29; see also comment on Lev. **14**.53).

The high priest, divested of his customary robes for the plainness of white linen, emphasized, by his appearance and by his ritual washings (4,24), the sole preoccupation at this stage with purification from sin (cf. Rev. **19**.8). After this, the 'glory and beauty' of his full attire (Exod. **28**.2) marked his return to his people to mediate in their sacrificial worship, even though the emphasis remained on its value for atonement (24).

The fulfilment far outstripped the foreshadowing, not only in the more radical divesting of the true High Priest and in His subsequent enthronement, 'crowned with glory and honour' (Heb. **2**.9; **10**.12), but in the value and efficacy of the sacrifice, made not 'once in the year '(34) but 'once for all' (Heb. **9**.12), and opening 'heaven itself' (Heb. **9**.24) to all the redeemed. And while the Aaronic high priest returned to his waiting people only to 'make atonement' immediately again with fresh sacrifices (24), the glory of the fulfilment is that Christ 'will appear a second time, sin done away, to bring salvation to those who are watching for Him' (Heb. **9**.28, NEB).

5. A HOLY NATION: Leviticus 17—27

Leviticus 17 — Precious Blood

That God is a jealous God—i.e. that there is no trifling with His Covenant nor with His prerogative as Creator—is made clear in two ways: by His concern for Israel's loyalty, and by His forbidding all invasion of His rights over life (exemplified here by blood). It is also clear that this attitude is love, both by the 'harlot' metaphor of v. 7 (cf. Paul's expansion of it in 2 Cor. **11**.2) and by the redemptive use which God assigns to the blood which He claims (11). These two concerns colour the two parts of the chapter.

No neglect of God's altar (1–9). To secularize a potential sacrifice, killing for private use an animal fit for a peace offering (1–4), is denounced as not only butchery but a step to treachery, since dues withheld from God are soon used against Him (7), and secularism is a vacuum waiting to be filled. The satyrs (7) were probably visualized as goat-like demons. Their cult reappears in 2 Chron. **11**.15 and perhaps 2 Kings **23**.8. If it resembled that of early Greece it was orgiastic.

The rule summed up in vs. 3 f. would no longer be practicable when Israel spread out over the promised land (see Deut. **12**.20 ff.), but that of vs. 8 f. continued in force (Deut. **12**.13 f.). Its neglect led to religious anarchy, as Hos. **8**.11 and the books of Kings reveal.

The sacredness of blood (10–16). The background to this legislation is as old as Noah (Gen. **9**.3–6); a standing reminder of man's limited rights over his fellow creatures. In the New Covenant the principle of both halves of this chapter are expected to be responsibly worked out in freedom (cf. 1 Cor. **10**.14–33).

Verse 11 is important for its clear statement of God's initiative in atonement. His 'I have given it for you' reverses the direction of flow that prevails in man-made religions, where the worshipper gives in order to receive. The background in Gen. **9**.3–6 and Exod. **21**.23 ('life for life') confirms that the shed blood is regarded here in its normal sense, as evidence of violent death, not (as some have tried to argue) as a store of quasi-magical vitality. This is expressed even more plainly if the last phrase is translated (as J. A. Motyer has suggested) 'at the cost of the life', as the Hebrew certainly allows; but it does not depend on any one translation. What this verse faintly foreshadows, the N.T. brings into full view, tirelessly proclaiming God's 'unspeakable gift' in 'the precious blood of Christ'.

Leviticus 18 — Sexual Sanity

The first and last paragraphs (1–5; 24–30), insisting that Israel must rise above heathen ways, enclose two blocks of sexual laws: on incest (6–18) and on other kinds of unchastity (19–23).

Verses 1–5. The refrain, 'I am the Lord your God', already found at **11**.45 and at the head of the Ten Commandments (Exod. **20**.2), opens and closes the chapter, and motivates the rest of the book (see especially ch. **19**). What *He is* must govern what we do. Its negative corollary, 'You shall not do as they do' (3), has its Christian equivalent everywhere in the epistles: e.g. Rom. **12**.2; 1 Cor. **6**.9–11, etc. In such a context the law of God is seen as the boon it ought to be; it is our inveterate sinfulness that has turned v. 5b into an accusation, as in Gal. **3**.12 (cf. Gal. **3**.21; Rom. **7**.10).

Verses 6–18. The ruling concern of these laws is not with genetics (although they are genetically beneficial), but with social decency. E.g., there is no blood tie between the would-be partners in vs. 14–18, but a family bond whose relationships must be kept distinct from those of sexual union. It develops the principle of Gen. **2**.24, where the same distinction is made for the protection of both marriage and the family. The prohibition in v. 16 is not in conflict with the law of levirate marriage (Deut. **25**.5 ff.), but refers to the (presumably divorced) wife of a living brother. Notice the improvement made in v. 18 over the customs that prevailed in Laban's circle (Gen. **29**.27), although the law still allowed polygamy, whose threats to family stability are reflected in several of these regulations and in the revealing word 'rival' (18).

Verses 19–23. The heinousness of these offences mounts with each example. That of v. 19 is treated as a minor offence in **15**.24, but as a major one in **20**.18, the difference evidently being between inadvertent and deliberate violations of the command. All the remainder, i.e. the sins of vs. 21–23, were capital offences; see ch. **20**. The children handed over to Molech (21) were possibly in some cases given to be temple prostitutes (the context of sexual sins and the absence of the words 'by fire' from the Hebrew here give some support to this), but there are other passages where it is clear that Molech received children as burnt offerings (e.g. 2 Kings **16**.3 with 2 Chron. **28**.3; Jer. **32**.35). The sharpest denunciations here ('abomination', 'perversion') are reserved for the deliberate depravities of vs. 22 f., a climax comparable to Rom. **1**.26 f.

Verses 24–30. The closing paragraph has the same basis as the opening one (see on vs. 1–5), but stiffens the commands with warnings. It is instructive to see various faces of judgement: as a divine act ('I am casting out . . .; I punished', 24 f.), as self-inflicted decline (they 'defiled themselves', 24, cf. v. 30), and as nature's retribution on the unnatural ('lest the land vomit you out', 28). To these, vs. 28 f. add an impressive note of impartiality, and Gen. **15**.13–16 one of unhurried progress to a just conclusion.

Leviticus 19 — Unclassified Ordinances

The unifying thread of the chapter is personal, namely the holy Lord Himself (2,3,4,10,12 . . .). That He had said a thing, was enough; one obeyed for His sake, not for one's own moral satisfaction. Jesus was to show that some aspects of the law, while all were binding, were 'weightier' than others—and yet were the very ones which tended to be neglected (Matt. **23**.23), since the legalist loves what he can measure.

All the major types of legislation meet in this miniature Pentateuch. The substance of six of the Ten Commandments is found in vs. 3,4,11,12; a sample of sacrificial law in vs. 5–8; Deuteronomy's concern for the poor and weak in vs. 9,10, 13,14, and its emphasis on the inward disposition in vs. 17,18; while an extreme example of technical purism in v. 19 rubs shoulders with the great commandment of v. 18 on the love of one's neighbour, which is given a searching interpretation, almost anticipating the Gospels, in v. 34. Other characteristic themes of the Law are equally prominent; it is instructive to make a list of them and of related passages in Exodus to Deuteronomy.

On matters of detail: v. 16 probably means giving false witness in a capital trial. In v. 17 note the same openness in dealing with a grievance as our Lord prescribed in Matt. **18.**15. In v. 20, Jewish tradition influenced the AV[KJV]'s unwarranted translation, 'she shall be scourged'. The RV's 'they shall be punished' also outruns the plain Hebrew, which is (cf. RSV) 'an inquiry shall be held'. In many civilizations inquiry has included torture (cf. Acts **22.**24), but the O.T. stands out in contrast, nowhere countenancing it.

In v. 23, 'forbidden' is literally 'uncircumcised'. Like the heathen, this was out of bounds; and even when this ban was lifted, the fruit must be for God before it could be for man. Sound farming, like sound hygiene in ch. **11**, was made a parable, and a vehicle of obedience and devotion. This is the method of the Law; its Christian equivalent, which should be no less thoroughgoing, is the maxim of 1 Cor. **10.**31. This motive prompts the obscurer as well as the plainer regulations of the remaining verses: e.g. vs. 27 f. refer to superstitious practices (possibly originating in attempts at self-disguise, for fear of spirits) unworthy of servants of the one Lord. His service may be exacting; it is also liberating: cf. Psa. **119.**45.

Leviticus 20 — Unclassified Ordinances (continued)

The brief law against the worship of Molech in **18.**21 is now expanded (1–5). God's name was 'profaned' (3; cf. **18.**21) not only by being linked, through His people, with such atrocities, but by the very notion that He should share His bride with others (cf. 'playing the harlot', 5c).

The name Molech almost certainly denotes a deity worshipped as king. It may be significant that other 'kingly' deities had to be similarly placated (2 Kings **17.**31b). It was part of God's justice that those who rebelled against His constructive kingship and laws should find themselves saddled with a tyrant and with 'statutes that were not good', fastened on them, as we should say, by the very logic of their choice (Ezek. **20.**23–26).

Stoning (2) appears to have been the standard form of execution (cf. John **8.**5 with Deut. **22.**22). It emphasized the people's corporate responsibility to administer God's sentence; it also brought home to the prosecution witnesses the gravity of their action, since they had to cast the first stones (Deut. **17.**7; cf. also Lev. **24.**14).

An apt comment on the prohibition of spiritualism (6) is the story of Saul, whose attempt to stamp out the practice confirms the antiquity of this law (1 Sam. **28**.3), and whose recourse to it in the end, when God was silent, brings out its character as an attempt to go behind God's back. The practice is consistently and vehemently condemned in the Law (Lev. **19**.31; Deut. **18**.11), and was punishable by death (v. 27; cf. Exod. **22**.18). Neither the cruelty perpetrated against innocent suspects in our own history, nor the existence of charlatans, alters the reality or the gravity of this offence against God.

Verses 10–27 continue to deal with matters already raised in earlier chapters. It is difficult to be certain of the distinctions between the terms 'cut off', 'bear his iniquity', and 'die childless' (see vs. 17–21 especially). The first of them may be a term for execution (cf. vs. 3–5), but its use elsewhere in purely ritual contexts points in those cases to banishment or excommunication (e.g. Lev. **7**.21,25,27). Perhaps the context determined the nature and duration of the sentence; in v. 17, etc. the similarity of the offences to those of vs. 10 ff. suggests the death penalty. 'Bear . . . iniquity' (17,19) might be paraphrased 'take the consequences'. 'Childless' (20 f.) is too precise a word to translate the Hebrew, since the latter (lit. 'stripped') has the meaning 'childless' in Gen. **15**.2 but not in Jer. **22**.30, where it indicates disgrace or destitution.

Notice again the guiding light of all these laws, in vs. 7,8,24,26. The heart of the covenant is expressed in v. 26c: 'that you should be Mine'. It is the sufficient reason for the high demands of the rest of the chapter and of the whole Law.

Questions for further study and discussion on Leviticus chs. 16—20

1. The notes on ch. **16** point out three aspects of atonement illustrated there: viz., access to God ('within'), the bearing of sin ('upon'), and its removal ('away'). Where in the Bible are these various aspects expounded more fully?
2. Blood, as life laid down, is said in **17**.11 to have special atoning value (cf. Heb. **9**.22). Collect and study the sayings of our Lord and of Heb. **9** and **10** on this.
3. The comment on **18**.24–30 speaks of the 'various faces of judgement'. Study these in conjunction with Gen. **3** and **4**, and with Rom. **1**.24–32.
4. Follow up the lines of study suggested in the second paragraph of the comments on ch. **19**.

Leviticus 21 Priestly Purity

The three paragraphs of this chapter point to an ideal of priesthood in which the private concerns of the priest are swallowed up in those of his ministry (1–15), and in which the sacrificer is as unblemished as the sacrifice (16–24, cf. **22**.19–25). The ideal is expressed in the clear-cut terms of outward practice and physique, which made the regulations workable while making at the same time the spiritual and moral implications very plain.

What was alien to God's holiness, whether technically (e.g. a corpse, 1 ff., 11) or morally (7,9), must be alien to those who would handle holy things, who could be defiled not only by contact (11) but by surrender—for that appears to underlie the mourning rites of vs. 5,10: by one's disfigured and dishevelled state one immersed oneself in the calamity. A priest, by contrast, especially the high priest (10), was reserved for God, and must be intact for Him. See also on **10**.4–7. Note that while the regulations of vs. 1–15 were without concessions, those of vs. 16–23, which were beyond a man's control, distinguished between the right to offer sacrifices and the right to partake of them (22). Fitness to mediate must be, by token, absolute; fitness to benefit was not by merit but by inheritance and grace.

The continuing relevance of the chapter derives from the twofold nature of the priesthood. (i) It was mediatorial, and pointed towards 'a high priest, holy, blameless, unstained' (Heb. **7**.26). This aspect of priesthood is fulfilled, without remainder, in Christ (Heb. **10**.11–14). (ii) It was a company of men called to a holiness whose constant demands overrode the 'changes and chances' of life, for the sake of others. This aspect is, or should be, fulfilled in the Church (cf. 1 Cor. **7**.29–31; Heb. **13**.15 f.; 1 Pet. **2**.9).

Notes: V. 4: 'as a husband' ('being a chief man', AV[KJV], RV): the abrupt Hebrew suggests a damaged text; there is no agreed solution. Ezek. **24**.16 f. tells against the RSV's translation here, since Ezekiel's behaviour was expected to appear startling, priest though he was. V. 10: 'hang loose': this is also the verb used of the people's disarray in Exod. **32**.25 and Prov. **29**.18. 'Nor rend his clothes': cf. Mark **14**.63.

Leviticus 22 More about Priests and Offerings

Various defilements (1–9). In contrast to the long-term disqualifications of ch. **21**, these are mostly brief and superficial. But they become serious (9) if they are taken lightly (note this principle: cf. Matt.

5.19), since the distinction between holy and profane is the great theme of these laws.

The priestly household (10–16). The principle here, as in, e.g. Exod. **12**.43–49, is that the privileges of the house are only for the committed, not for those who have a foot in another establishment (as in vs. 10,12). So the slave has the advantage in this respect over the free man. The inclusion of the priest's household at his table is no relaxing of the law, as vs. 14–16 re-emphasize; notice the responsibility of the priests to see that holy things are not cheapened and thereby made a source of guilt (14–16).

Unblemished victims (17–25). Priest and sacrifice alike were to be perfect specimens: see **21**.16–23; cf. Heb. **9**.14, where 'Christ . . . offered Himself without blemish to God'. The obvious importance that a sacrifice 'be accepted . . .' (19) is not forgotten by Paul in Rom. **12**.1 f., speaking of the Christian's acceptable self-offering; contrast the grudging sacrifices of Mal. **1**.8 ff. As regards the degree of imperfection tolerable in a freewill offering (23), A. Bonar points out that such a gift reflects the offerer's sense of gratitude, inadequate as it is, rather than God's atoning provision, and he contrasts the narrowness of the former with the breadth of the latter (*A Commentary on Leviticus*, p. 390). In v. 24, translate the last clause 'You are not to do that in your country' (Jerusalem Bible; cf. RV)—i.e. not use these methods, nor (25) offer such animals bought from foreigners. Holiness, with its rejection of a 'maimed or worthless sacrifice', went hand in hand here with mercy (cf. the law against human castration, Deut. **23**.1).

Calves and lambs (26–30). Here again, ritual and humane considerations seem to unite in motivating these regulations. With the provision of v. 28, cf. Exod. **23**.19b, which may be a counterblast to fertility magic; but cf., too, such simple restraints on human callousness as those of Deut. **22**.1–4, 6–8, etc.

The unifying theme: holiness (31–33). The petition 'hallowed be Thy name' would express the aim of each part of this law. For the Christian this prayer has implications that are no less multiform, and no less searching.

Leviticus 23 — The Sacred Calendar

This chapter has its complement in Num. **28,29**, which prescribes the sacrifices for these (and other) occasions. To the Christian it is remarkable for God's seal on its main outline, in the Gospel events. 'Christ our Passover' (1 Cor. **5**.7) was sacrificed during the feast of that name, against all human attempts to avoid that period (Matt. **26**.5). 'Christ the first fruits' (1 Cor. **15**.20,23) was raised 'on the morrow after the sabbath', the day of presenting the first fruits (Lev. **23**.10)—for the sabbath in question was that of the passover, from which the feast of Pentecost, meaning the fiftieth day, was reckoned (15 f. cf. Acts **2**.1). Pentecost itself (15–21), at which the first harvest of the gospel age (John **12**.24; Acts **2**.41) coincided with the O.T. wheat festival, was again a time of God's choosing, not man's. Finally, the N.T. uses the symbol of the vintage, the final ingathering (39–43, cf. Exod. **34**.22), for the coming judgement of the world (Rev. **14**.18, cf. Rev. **19**.15). But in both Testaments this event is dominated by the theme of liberation (40,43; Rev. **15**.3 f.).

Significantly, the Day of Atonement (26–32, cf. ch. **16**) has left no comparable mark on the N.T. except in the comparisons drawn between its limitations and the perfection of the work of Christ. See the points of contrast in Heb. **9,10**.

Notes: V. 3: 'a holy convocation': this is one of the few, but sufficient, specific indications in the O.T. that the sabbath was prescribed for public worship as well as rest. V. 5 (margin): 'between the two evenings': i.e. probably, between sunset and nightfall. V. 22: neighbourly love breaks in, amongst the technicalities, cf. **19**.9 f. V. 32: 'from evening to evening': this reckoning probably does not spring from Gen. **1**.5 (which states that evening drew on, not that it began the day) but from the concern to prepare for the morrow.

Leviticus 24 — Unbroken Homage

The sanctuary light (1–4). The force of the word 'continually' is limited by the phrase 'from evening to morning' (3). I.e., the lamp was to burn by night without fail, but apparently not through the day. Cf. Exod. **30**.7 f.; 1 Sam. **3**.3.

The imagery of the lampstand reappears in Zech. **4**.2 ff. and in Rev. **1**.12,20; **2**.5; in both of which places it portrays the Church, though there is little hint of this here. Situated outside the veil but within the tent, accessible to the priests alone, it served the ends of worship (cf. Psa. **134**.1) rather than witness, along with the altar of incense (cf. Psa. **141**.2; Rev. **5**.8) and the table of showbread which stood with it. The N.T. balances this by calling the Church to bring its light out of seclusion (Matt. **5**.14–16; Phil. **2**.15).

The showbread (5–9). This 'bread of (God's) presence' was placed on a table that was plated with gold and laid with golden dishes, spoons, flagons and bowls (Exod. **25**.23–30), a display fit to suggest a banquet in His honour. But the plain food prescribed as the offering spoke of His concern not for the exotic and elaborate, but simply for a complete Israel (cf. the twelve loaves) presented to Him in order (6), purity and perpetuity.

A blasphemer and the law of retribution (10–23). The ugly incident of vs. 10 ff. jarring against the theme of 'holy' and 'most holy' (9) makes a pointed comment on the human material available. Moses' refusal, however, to be hurried into a decision (12) is instructive in itself; it also emphasizes the divine authority of the ensuing death sentence. The law of retribution (17–22), reaffirmed from Exod. **21**.23 ff., upheld the principle of an equivalent as against an arbitrary penalty. It is important to realize, first, that the law itself used the principle flexibly (see Exod. **21**.26 f.), and secondly that the N.T. condemns its use, not in the context of public law (cf. Rom. **13**.3 f.), but in that of personal relations (Rom. **12**.19; Matt. **5**.38 ff.).

As a postscript, the deaths of Jesus and Stephen for blasphemy show what happens when a just law falls into the hands of the prejudiced—those whose religion finds expression in the words 'they stopped their ears and rushed together . . .' (Acts **7**.57).

Leviticus 25 — Sabbatical Year and Jubilee

The Jerusalem Bible divides the chapter (preferably to RSV) after v. 22, analysing the second portion as 'Consequences of the holiness of land and people', with the subtitles 'a. The land: redemption of landed property' (23–34), and 'b. The people: loans and enfranchisement' (35–55).

Verses 1–22. However sound the principle of a fallow year, it would invite disaster to observe it everywhere simultaneously (as the chapter seems to require), but for the divine promise of vs. 20–22 (cf. **26**.10). The jubilee, with two fallow years in succession (11), intensified the test of faith to an extreme; for the whole ordinance meant taking one's hands off the most basic things of life, to concede that they were primarily God's. This was too much for pre-exilic Israel, whose land had to wait for the captivity to enjoy its sabbaths (**26**.34 f.; 2 Chron. **36**.21).

Verses 23–55. The basis of the law that made property inalienable was not the rights of man but the crown rights of God ('the land is Mine', 23), which were incidentally a man's best protection. It was no accident that Naboth lost his vineyard to a king who had lost his faith (1 Kings **21**; cf. Isa. **5**.8,12). As well as limiting what money could buy, the emphasis on God's primacy raised the question of how money should be made and spent (35–38), and whose servants, ultimately, were the men you seemed to own ('For they are My servants' 42,55). (On the economics of v. 37, see on Deut. **23**.19 f.). Where the law discriminates between Israelite and foreign slaves

(45 f.), it does so by stressing the special generosity due to a 'brother' (35,36,39, etc.), not by disparaging the stranger or refusing him legal status (see Lev. **24**.22). If the N.T. goes far beyond this (Gal. **3**.28), the O.T. has already made a notable beginning.

On the relation of this law of slavery to that of Exod. **21**.2 ff. and Deut. **15**.12 ff., evidently there was a distinction between those whose slavery was enforced for theft or debt and those who took refuge in it for security (39; cf. A. H. Finn, *The Unity of the Pentateuch*, pp. 169 f.), contracting for a potentially longer term of service, but a better status (39 f.) and an option of redemption at any time (48 f.).

Leviticus 26 — A Concluding Charge to Israel

This appeal was to be echoed, forty years later, in the parting words of Moses, where its substance is re-shaped into the blessings and cursings that clinch a covenant.

The basic loyalty (1,2). The decalogue opens with the same emphasis as this, in its four Godward commandments, which Israel's subsequent history shows to have been the crucial issue for her (see, e.g. Hos. **4** for the social effects of her wavering allegiance).

The blessings of obedience (3–13). The good things of this paragraph are only marginally the ordinary fruits of sound living. Going far beyond natural achievement, it is God's ordering, protecting, conquering, fertilizing, and liberating presence that is the special promise of these verses. Note the assurance that is the essence of salvation, in vs. 12 f. (cf. Rev. **21**.3); note, too, the striking close: '. . . and made you walk erect'; cf. Psa. **40**.2.

The pains of disobedience (14–46). There is a controlled crescendo of divine wrath revealed here. The repeated 'sevenfold' (18,21,24,28), the lengthening paragraphs, the deepening disasters (whose climax lies beyond even the cannibalism of v. 29, in the utter demoralization of vs. 36–39) are held nevertheless within the strong framework of God's forbearance, seen in the search for signs of repentance (14a, 21a,23,27), in the limited duration, implied in the phrase 'as long as' (34 f.), and in the assurance that the ancient covenant will survive (44 f.). The humbling contrast between man and God shows clearly in the parallel phrases: 'they spurned My ordinances . . . Yet . . . I will not spurn them' (43 f.).

Note: The expression 'enjoy its sabbaths' (34,43) should perhaps be rendered 'fulfil . . .' etc., since the verb is that of v. 43b, 'make amends', where it expresses the idea of satisfying a creditor. A similar vocabulary is used in Isa. **40**.2. On these 'sabbaths', see on **25**.1 ff.

The assessment of vows (1–25). The money values in this chapter were laid down to enable a gift in kind to be replaced by one in cash with some degree of realism.

(i) *People* (1–8). An example of such a vow is Hannah's offering of Samuel, although hers was irrevocable (1 Sam. **1**.11). The sliding scale was concerned with approximate economic, not spiritual, values; it reflected something of the actualities as one presented to God possibly the 'fag-end' or possibly the full strength of a life; so it guarded against hypocrisy, while leaving room for hard cases (8). The truth that all are fundamentally equal before God is expressed elsewhere, in the law that assessed each person's 'ransom' at a mere half-shekel, regardless of wealth (Exod. **30**.11–16).

(ii) *Animals* (9–13), (iii) *Houses* (14 f.), (iv) *Land* (16–25). Here again the concern is partly to combat hypocrisy (10a), vacillation (10b) and wrangling (12), but partly, too, to clarify the relation of vows to the laws on landholding and the jubilee (16–25).

Special cases (26–33). With the notion that one can put God in one's debt with what is already His (26,30), compare Luke **17**.10; 1 Cor. **4**.7. The meaning of 'devoted' (28 f.) is quite distinct from 'dedicated' or 'vowed', being a special word for the things and people due for extermination (cf. Jericho) by a divine decree. It was this command that Achan and King Saul tried to circumvent.

The tithe (30–33) was no innovation: Jacob had vowed it to God at Bethel (Gen. **28**.22), and Abram had tithed his battle spoils to Melchizedek as priest (Gen. **14**.19 f.). The N.T., finally, adds its own reminders (to those that are implicit in this chapter) that a legalistic spirit can misuse the best of laws. See our Lord's comments on cash assessments in Matt. **23**.16–22, on tithing in Matt. **23**.23, and on twisted vows in Matt. **15**.4–9.

Questions for further study and discussion on Leviticus chs. 21—27

1. From the contexts in which 'holy' is used in these chapters (and in chs. **17** ff.) what are the chief implications of this word?
2. God's acts of creation and redemption underlie the round of festivals in ch. **23**. Has this anything to teach the Christian about patterns of worship, or has the N.T. left such a scheme entirely behind?
3. What lessons about material wealth can we learn from ch. **25**?
4. What insight does ch. **26** give us into the ways of God and man?

Numbers

OUTLINE

1. THE PILGRIMS MARSHALLED: chs. 1—4

1 The Census
2 Israel in Array
3, 4 The Tribe of Levi

2. MISCELLANEOUS DIRECTIVES: chs. 5, 6

3. THE TABERNACLE SERVICE INAUGURATED: chs. 7.1—10.10

4. THE MARCH RESUMED AND HALTED: chs. 10.11—14.45

10.11–36 As an Army with Banners
11 Discontent
12 Disunity at the Top
13 The Reconnaissance
14 The Great Refusal

5. FURTHER LAWS AND LAWLESSNESS: chs. 15—19

15 Ritual Additions and Clarifications
16 The Rebellion of Korah
17 The Sign of Aaron's Rod
18 Priests' and Levites' Responsibilities and Rewards
19 The Ashes of a Heifer

6. FINAL JOURNEYS AND ENCOUNTERS: chs. 20.1—33.49

20, 21 Spiritual Failures, Physical Conquests
22 The Hiring of Balaam
23, 24 The Oracles of Balaam
25 Disaster at Peor
26 The Second Census
27 Two Problems of Continuity
28, 29 The Calendar of Offerings
30 Responsibility for Vows
31 Vengeance against Midian
32 'Do not take us across the Jordan'
33.1–49 The Log of the Journey

7. THE PROSPECT OF CANAAN: chs. 33.50—36.13

33.50—34.29 Realistic Planning
35 Special Cities
36 A Problem of Inheritance

1. THE PILGRIMS MARSHALLED: Numbers 1—4

* Numbers 1 — The Census

The events of the opening chapters are dated a month after the erection of the tabernacle (Exod. **40**.17), and a fortnight after the first wilderness passover, recorded in Num. **9**. The census is a military one (3,20,22, etc.), setting the tone of this book, in which Israel, seen in the Book of Exodus mainly as a liberated people, and in Leviticus as a consecrated people, is faced now with fighting its way into its inheritance—a task it will initially refuse.

The military emphasis may have left its mark on the method of numbering the tribes, where it has been variously conjectured that the word for thousands may have originally meant in this context 'clans' (as in Judg. **6**.15), 'officers' (cf. Zech. **9**.7, AV[KJV], RV), 'trained men' (from a verb to learn), or 'military units' (cf. Num. **31**.14, where 'hundreds' might stand for similar but smaller units). Possibly such military companies were numbered by their nominal value rather than their current strength. The subject is discussed by J. W. Wenham, 'Large Numbers in the Old Testament', *Tyndale Bulletin* **18** (1967), pp. 19–53.

Verses 47–54. The Levites, exempt from soldiering, had an indispensable role as mediators (53). Negatively, compare vs. 51,53 with the sharp lessons of 1 Sam. **6**.19 f.; 1 Chron. **13**.9 f.; **15**.2 ff.; positively, compare this living wall between tent and people (53) with the shield of intercession when Moses 'stood in the breach . . . to turn away (God's) wrath' (Psa. **106**.23), or when he was stationed to intercede above the battle in Exod. **17**.8–13. On such apparent inessentials 'hung the issue of the day', then as now.

* Numbers 2 — Israel in Array

Two things plainly emerge from this chapter: the value set on good order, and the centrality given to God. As to the first, clearly there was, and is, much to be gained in efficiency by eliminating uncertainty and the friction of jockeying for position; yet the smooth running could still conceal deep jealousies (cf., e.g. Judg. **12**.1–6; 2 Sam. **19**.43). Note that our Lord refrained from fixing a similar 'seating order' among His twelve, preferring to educate them by exposing their rivalries and expounding the ultimate realities of rank (e.g. Mark **9**.33 ff.; **10**.35 ff.).

God's centrality was symbolized not only in camp, where the tent of meeting, surrounded by the tribe of Levi, was the focus of the inward-facing square formed by the twelve other tribes (2), but also on the march, where the holy things and their bearers were assigned to the mid-point of the line (17). An incidental effect of such a pattern of march was to distribute responsibility, since the honour of forming the vanguard or rearguard was matched by that of constituting the central bodyguard to the tabernacle and its treasures.

God 'in the midst' (cf. v. 17) is a recurrent topic in Scripture, seen from afar in the ideal pattern of Israel in Ezekiel's vision (Ezek. **43.**7; **48.**35); encamped among us, unrecognized, in the Incarnation (John **1.**14); present in the assembled church (Matt. **18.**20); and visible in full glory in the new creation (Rev. **21.**3; **22.**3), where the pattern of the desert camp of Israel reappears, transfigured, in that of the twelve-gated city of God (Rev. **21.**12–14). See also on **5.**1–4.

* Numbers 3 — The Tribe of Levi

(i) *The priests* (1–4). The death of Nadab and Abihu for sacrilege is recounted in Lev. **10,** where Eleazar and Ithamar are shown taking over their duties at once (Lev. **10.**12 ff., 16 ff.), so vital was the role of mediator. Of the two families, Ithamar's had gained the primacy by Eli's day, but abused its trust and was subordinated again to the elder branch (cf. 1 Sam. **2.**30 ff.; 1 Kings **2.**26 f.).

(ii) *The Levites, in relation to the priests* (5–10) *and to Israel* (11–13). The two words, 'given' (9) and 'Mine' (12), express the exacting vocation of the Levites, at once lowly and lofty—a fair sample of all divine service. Chapter **8** will describe their initiation into their new office

(iii) *The numbering and division of the Levites* (14–39). In the next chapter fuller details are given of the duties of the three branches of the tribe. Here we may note that children, from a month upward (15, etc.), were numbered among the consecrated (cf. vs. 40 ff.), although they would not do actual service before thirty (**4.**3,23, etc.) or, for some duties, twenty-five (**8.**24).

[N.B. (*i*) The fact that the Amramites were already a clan (27) suggests that Amram was a distant rather than an immediate progenitor of Moses (Exod. **6.**18,20). This agrees with other chronological data and with genealogical conventions.

(*ii*) In v. 28 the Septuagint's 8,300 corrects a scribal slip whereby a 3 had evidently become a 6 by the omission of one letter (cf. the total, v. 39)].

Note the precision of the camping stations, with the four sides of the tabernacle each flanked by its particular group (23,29,35,38), so that priests and Levites made a camp within a camp, interposed between their brethren and divine judgement (cf. **1**.53).

(iv) *The Levites as substitutes for the firstborn* (40–51). The emphasis throughout this passage, on God's unconditional claim on the lives concerned, should counteract the notion that man gratuitously confers upon God his vote or his service. With the claiming of the firstborn, compare that of the Christian's whole family: 'Otherwise, your children would be unclean, but as it is they are holy' (1 Cor. **7**.14).

On the assessment of the firstborn's redemption, i.e. the price of release from service, cf. the note on Lev. **27**.1–8. Here, their involuntary obligation is assessed at a 'flat rate' corresponding to the lowest of the charges in the former passage, where a contract had been freely entered into.

* Numbers 4 — The Tribe of Levi (continued)

(v) *The duties of the clans* (1–33). These tasks have already been broadly indicated in **3**.25,29–31,36 f. The details that are now filled in help to emphasize the unapproachable holiness of the sanctuary. If the tribe of Levi had to insulate Israel from exposure to the tabernacle (**1**.53), the priests must shield the Levites themselves against contact with what it contained. After the instructions for covering the holy vessels (5–15), v. 20 clinches the object-lesson with perhaps the strongest warning in the whole law on the lethal impact of holiness on the intruder. This (with v. 15b) is the context of the judgement on the men of Bethshemesh and on Uzzah (1 Sam. **6**.19; 1 Chron. **13**.10), when these warnings were found to be more than words. David's reaction to the second incident, passing from anger and fear to obedience and joy (1 Chron. **13**.11 f.; **15**.2–15, 25–29), shows how unpalatable but how potentially fruitful is God's rebuke to man's casualness.

(vi) *The census of serving Levites* (34–49). The qualifying age of thirty refers to the duty of carrying the tabernacle and its vessels. Liturgical duties began at twenty-five (**8**.24). At a later stage, when there was no longer a portable tabernacle, David redesigned and enlarged the pattern of Levitical service, and brought forward the starting age to twenty (1 Chron. **23**.24–27).

2. MISCELLANEOUS DIRECTIVES: Numbers 5,6

Numbers 5 — 'None of us lives to himself'

Expulsion of the unclean (1–4). Fuller instructions on uncleanness are given elsewhere (Lev. **13**.45 f.; **15**.2 ff.; Num. **19**.11 ff.): here they are put into effect, and their basis explained in v. 3b (which is the basis of all holy living).

Restitution, and priestly dues (5–10). The expression 'breaking faith' (6) is the same as that used of marital infidelity in vs. 12,27 since our Godward relationship has much in common with marriage. It is striking that a wrong done to a fellow man is viewed first and foremost as done against God (see on Lev. **6**.1–7).

The accused wife (11–31). This is the nearest approach in Scripture to a trial by ordeal, a favourite procedure in ancient times. But it differs crucially from most of these trials, first, by looking not to the potion itself but primarily to the Lord (21) for the verdict, and secondly, by requiring a demonstration of guilt rather than of innocence. (Generally in such trials the accused was tested with something deadly, but here with nothing physically potent enough to cause the drastic damage of v. 22.)

The test was by exposure to holiness: holy water, holy ground (17) and, placed in the woman's own hands, an 'offering of remembrance' (15b), i.e. an offering that lodged an appeal to God for action against sin.

The ritual, like all Biblical rites, would take effect not automatically as if by magic, but as the instrument of God's will in accordance with truth. The curse would not operate unjustly (Prov. **26**.2), but it could not be side-stepped, with its writing made an ingredient of the potion (note incidentally this early use, apparently, of parchment and ink, 23) and its terms accepted with the double Amen (22).

But vindicated or not, the accused wife could only be deeply humiliated (see, e.g. v. 18) and the marital relationship violently strained by such a procedure (to which, characteristically, tradition was to add further degradations). Whether a husband resorted to it or not depended on the man he was (cf. Matt. **1**.19). But the existence of such a law could leave no doubt of the extreme gravity of adultery in the eyes of God. As a postscript, in case the male should suppose himself entitled to more lenient divine judgement, see Hos. **4**.14 (RSV).

Numbers 6 — The Nazirite Vow

The ruling idea of the term 'Nazirite' comes out in the kindred words translated 'separate', 'separation', 'consecrated' (18) and 'consecration' (19) in this chapter, all from the root *n-z-r*. The Nazirite was set apart from some aspects of normal life, to be more conspicuously available for God. The negative and positive sides are shown in the three abstentions and in the clinching verse, v. 8.

The vine (3 f.) was one of the minor luxuries of settled life, in contrast to the simple fare of the nomad (cf. Jer. 35.6 f,). The unshorn hair (5) may have had the symbolism found in Exod. 20.25; Deut. 15.19, where things set apart for God must be given Him intact. Ceremonial cleanness (6 f.) was the precondition for worship, and the Nazirite must be as constantly ready as the high priest himself (cf. v. 7 with Lev. 21.1–3,11). The vow could be lifelong (cf. Samson, Samuel, John the Baptist) or temporary (cf. Paul in Acts 18.18, and the four men of Acts 21.23–28; the latter seem to have been carrying out the conditions of vs. 9 ff.).

All of this bore special witness to the pilgrim spirit and the self-dedication and purity of life which were fundamentally the calling of every Israelite. It is worth noting that while this vow was to be treated most seriously (cf. Samson's tragedy; see also Amos 2.11 ff.), it was a particular expression of holiness that was not required of everyone, nor a matter of extra merit, as Matt. 11.18 f. proves.

The priestly blessing (22–27). The explanatory v. 27 is important, and is further illuminated by, e.g. Exod. 20.24b, where God promises to meet His people with blessing wherever He records His name. The inclusive term, 'bless' (23), is expounded by its companion words, ranging from protection (24) to the concord which is the positive content of 'peace' (26). But the dominant note is personal, with the varied expressions in vs. 25,26a for enjoying not only God's benefits but His smile.

Questions for further study and discussion on Numbers chs. 1—6

1. Look up the references to God 'in the midst', in the final comment on ch. 2, and find further examples and developments of this theme.
2. 'They shall not . . . look upon the holy things even for a moment, lest they die' (4.20). If this was the fate of an intruder (see notes), study the similarities and differences in the reception given to a genuine seeker (e.g. Gen. 32.24 ff.; Exod. 33.18 ff.; Isa. 6; 2 Cor. 3.18; etc.).
3. 'The spirit of jealousy' (5.14). This is the same word as 'zeal', and can be used in a good or a bad sense. Study this word in Scripture, and pinpoint the good qualities of which the bad ones are a corruption.
4. Discuss the bearing, if any, of the Nazirite's special vocation (see second paragraph of Notes on ch 6) on the varied patterns of Christian living. How relevant is 1 Cor. 7 (e.g. vs. 7 ff., 17 ff.) to this?

3. THE TABERNACLE SERVICE INAUGURATED: Numbers 7.1—10.10

Numbers 7 — The Best for God

The gift of wagons (1–9). This presentation, to greet the erection of the tabernacle, was clearly a voluntary gesture, taking Moses by surprise (4 f.). It is worth observing both the passive and the active role of Moses in receiving divine guidance about it, in that he waited for God's will to be made plain (4–6)—since not every human offer is serviceable for His work; and that he took care to think out the apportionment of the gifts so as to comply with his existing instructions (7,8, especially 9; cf. ch.4)—thereby avoiding the well-meaning blunders of David and others as in 2 Sam. 6.3 ff.

The offerings for the altar (10–88). The twelve identical offerings, furnishing the altar with the main requirements for worship, gave every tribe an equal share in what would be done and offered there; and the twelve days (11) led up towards the climax on the fourteenth: the first Passover since Egypt (cf. Exod. 40.17; Num. 7.10; 9.1–3).

The voice from the Mercy Seat (89). While God had many ways of speaking (e.g. 12.6 ff.), certainly plain, audible utterance was one of them (cf. the boy Samuel's experience: 1 Sam. 3.4 ff.). As to the place from which the voice was heard, the description makes it clear that God was not contained or embodied in the ark or cherubim, but enthroned on and attended by them (cf. Pss. 80.1; 99.1, etc.); and the terms of the verse are reminders of the conditions of a divine-human meeting: namely, atonement (the basic meaning of 'mercy seat') and covenant (the significance of the 'testimony' in this phrase; cf. 10.33, etc.), whereby the militant holiness signified by the cherubim (cf. Gen. 3.24; Ezek. 10.2) is turned to man's salvation instead of his destruction (Psa. 18.6–19).

Numbers 8 — The Living Flame

The seven lamps lit (1–4). On the symbolism of the lampstand in Scripture, see on Lev. 24.1–4. Some idea of 'the pattern' of it (4) can be gathered from the bas-relief on the Arch of Titus in Rome, where the Temple's lampstand is shown among the spoils captured from Jerusalem in A.D. 70. By then, as Heb. 8.5; 9.2,23 f. explain, the earthly sanctuary and its furniture had been superseded by the realities they portrayed.

The living sacrifice (5–26). This occasion may have been in Paul's mind in the writing of Rom. 12.1, where, as here, the prelude to the living sacrifice is seen to be atonement and the discarding of the old life (cf. v. 7 with e.g. Rom. 6.3 f.). On the expression 'wave offering' (11), see on Lev. **7**.28–36; the Levites may have been led to the altar and back to their place. The act of laying hands on them (10) has an important bearing on the theology of sacrifice, since v. 16 (with its phrase, 'instead of') makes it clear that the Levites were offered as substitutes for their fellows. The gesture that signified this was repeated immediately afterwards, when the Levites, for their part, laid their hands on the animals that were to be their sin offering and burnt offering (12).

Another matter clarified here is the term 'consecrated' (17), and its companion words 'sanctified', 'holy', etc., which represent the same Hebrew root. It is used here to sum up a group of non-technical terms which display its different facets: e.g. 'separate(d)', 'Mine' (14), 'wholly given' (16; lit., 'given, given'), 'taken' (18). It emerges from the same context that God is generous with what He takes. 'I have taken' (18) is closely followed by 'I have given' (19). The Levites were withdrawn from one sphere to serve in another (where a greater variety of work awaited them than appears from this passage by itself: cf. 1 Chron. **23—26**; 2 Chron. **17**.8 f.; **19**.8). Even after retirement they were to reckon that they could still be of use (25 f.). And the Church continues to profit from the many psalms which are the legacy of Asaphites and Korahites (e.g. Pss. **73–85**), sons of Levi.

Numbers 9.1—10.10 Worshippers, Pilgrims, Warriors

The second Passover (**9**.1–14). The difference in kind between the first and all subsequent Passovers would be especially vivid on this occasion, when memories of the night of judgement and liberation were fresh. *Then*, salvation had been in the making, now it was a fact to build on, and the feast was kept not to ensure it but to celebrate it: cf. Exod. **13**.8.

The supplementary law recorded in vs. 6–14 was invoked in Hezekiah's day, and was stretched still further at the king's intercession (2 Chron. **30**.2 ff., 18–20)—an incident which confirms the impression given here of a régime that was merciful and adaptable, for all its intolerance of the arrogant and the careless. The incident is one of several that show the development of the law, as new matters came up for decision; but Moses' humility (8; cf. note on **7**.1–9) ensured that this case-law was as divinely authorized as the basic statutes.

The cloud and fire (**9**.15–23). This token of God's presence came to be known as the Shekinah, from a verb 'to dwell'. It had been visible at the first stage of the Exodus (Exod. **13**.21; **14**.19), and its presence now above the tabernacle showed that God accepted this as

'My house' rather than 'your house' (cf. Matt. **21**.13; **23**.38). In the cloud's removing or resting (17 ff.), Christians may still see an expressive metaphor for the guidance they can expect, in the quiet indications of God's will for their movements.

The silver trumpets (**10**.1–10). These, or their successors, are portrayed on the Arch of Titus, with the table of showbread and the lampstand (see on **8**.1–4), and were distinct from the rams' horn (*shophar* or *yobel*) sounded at, e.g. the battle of Jericho or the year of jubilee. Their military function (like that of bugles), to call the camp to specific action, seems to have determined their symbolic use as a call to God to rally to His people (9b). The same thought, but without the overtones of danger, is implied in the trumpet call at sacrifices and festivals, as if to say 'Lord, come to us!' (10). The 'trumpets and . . . horn' of Psa. **98**.6 are of more than musical significance: they voice the nations' jubilant prayer.

So this paragraph appropriately rounds off the inauguration of the tabernacle, and looks ahead to action, as Israel prepares to march, to fight and to feast.

4. THE MARCH RESUMED AND HALTED; Numbers 10.11—14.45

Numbers 10.11–36 — As an Army with Banners

The order of march (11–28). Israel had been encamped at Sinai for nearly a year (11; cf. Exod. **19**.1), attending to the priorities: law, covenant, worship, community. Without these, Canaan would be a second Egypt. But the march, too, was a preparation, a training in orderly co-operation, as here, in readiness for the campaign, and an exercise in walking by faith. It was a demanding mixture of routine and unpredictability, such as God may still prescribe for the pilgrim.

The means of guidance (29–36). The general guiding of Israel by the cloud was no substitute for local knowledge. Moses, for all his years in Midian, was not desert-bred, and, to his credit, knew his limitations and the value of an expert's eye for detail (31). In time to come, his welcome for a genuine ally would not go unrewarded: cf. Judg. **5**.24 ff.

The stirring invocation at the beginning and end of journeys (35 f.) pictures the Lord as ranging ahead of His people, clearing a path for them. Note that the second prayer does not visualize Him as confined to the vicinity of the ark, for this merely halts and the people gather round it; whereas the Lord returns from the fray, to station Himself again in the midst. Psa. **68**, which opens with the prayer of our v. 35, magnificently develops the theme of the march of God, not only through the deserts but through the skies (Psa. 68.4,33), and of His enthronement at the sanctuary, which becomes the centre of not only Israel but the world.

Numbers 11 — Discontent, and Coals of Fire

To take part in the greatest expedition in history and to be obsessed with the diet, was to be ludicrously small-minded. Apart from Moses and a few others, these men revealed themselves to be no pilgrims, but only refugees like their camp followers (4; cf. Exod. **12**.38). Even the least visionary of them might have foreseen a certain scarcity of fish (5)! But the N.T. advises us to view these chapters less as a casebook than as, potentially, a mirror (1 Cor. **10**.6), and it has its own tale of similar incongruities to add (e.g. Mark **9**.31–34; 1 Cor. **11**.20 f.), which present-day Christians, if they searched their hearts, could supplement. As to the manna (7–9; cf. Exod. **16**.14 ff.), human perversity disdained a food which was nevertheless pleasant, versatile (8) and a gift from God (Exod. **16**.15)—just as it would disdain, eventually, the Bread of Life (John **6**.35 ff.).

Verses 10 ff. reveal something of the strain of Moses' isolation, which had brought him to the verge of breakdown. To the overwrought, God is understanding and constructive: there is no rebuke for Moses' tirade, or even for the scepticism of vs. 21 f.; only the practical answer of the double intervention (16 f., 18–20). The sending of the quails is a classic example of judgement by a surfeit of the thing one has craved. The enduing of the seventy elders with the Spirit raises the interesting question of their relation to the leaders chosen in Exod. **18**.24 ff. and to the seventy elders of Exod. **24**.9–11. If the three groups are identical (cf. the wording of v.16) it may imply that the attempt to share responsibility had broken down through spiritual disunity, of which Eldad and Medad's absenting themselves was a sample. The true remedy was to partake of the same Spirit (the Lord's, 29b), whose bestowal on this special occasion was marked by a temporary sign (25c,d) possibly like that of Pentecost. Moses' reply to the zealous Joshua (28 f.) is a model for every leader, and has good reason to be called Christlike: cf. Luke **9**.49 f.

Numbers 12 — Disunity at the Top

With the deviousness of malice, Miriam and Aaron dressed up their rancour as religious principle. To have objected openly to the newcomer would have been an admission of simple jealousy, so the single point of contact between the actual (1) and the pretended issue (2), namely the person of Moses, was made their target. The fact that Miriam is named before Aaron and was the only one to be punished, suggests that it was she who resented the new 'first lady' (1) and was the instigator of the attack, manipulating the pliant Aaron, who had once before shown himself susceptible to the suggestion that his talents were wasted (Exod. 32.1).

The 'meekness' of Moses (3) was not a matter of temperament (cf. Exod. 2.11 f.) but of subordinating his personal interests to those of God and His cause, leaving his vindication in God's hands, like the true Servant in Isa. 50.5–7. A less misleading adjective would be 'humble'. In passing, the bearing of this verse (3) on the authorship of the book is no different from that of the 'he' which is used everywhere of Moses in these narratives except where he is spoken to or speaking (e.g. 11.11 ff. and most of Deut.). I.e., the books of Moses were compiled from his own written records (cf. Deut. 31.24), but in the form of biography, not autobiography.

In vindicating Moses, God dealt first with the slander, which had been that convenient alloy, a half-truth (Moses was unique in responsibility and intimacy [7 f.], not in prophetic function), and after that, with the slanderers (9 ff.). It is instructive that the high praise of v. 7 is used in Heb. 3.2–6 to show how far he himself is surpassed by Christ. It is the difference between steward and son: cf. Gen. 15.2–5.

On Miriam's 'leprosy', and the phrase 'white as snow', see on Lev. 13. Moses' intercession for her (13) was wholly in character: cf. 11.2; 14.13 ff.; etc. In this respect, too, he showed the mark of the great Servant (Isa. 53.12c), which is also the badge of His household (Matt. 5.44; 1 Pet. 3.9).

Numbers 13 — The Reconnaissance

The fact that God was the commander of the enterprise might have seemed to make this survey superfluous. But the searching questions of vs. 17–20 make it clear that He does not excuse His servants the normal burdens of fact-finding, value-judgement and responsible decision. His army must not be one of conscripts or passengers, but of volunteers who have espoused His cause and counted the cost; it is the only way for omnipotence to work alongside finite men without swamping them. (Those who 'play at God' sometimes forget how He does it Himself.)

Accordingly we find every tribe represented (1–16), the whole length of the land inspected, and the rough taken faithfully with the smooth: the gigantic grape-cluster (23) matched the news of less inviting giants. There can be no subsequent complaint of a blind choice.

The sequel illustrates the diametrically opposite assessments ('well able', 'not able', vs. 30 f.) which can be made of exactly the same data; for the visible facts were not yet in dispute, only the invisible—and these not explicitly, at this stage. Caleb (soon to be joined openly by Joshua: **14**.6 ff.) exemplifies the realism of the spiritually minded, in viewing the picture in its frame, the will of God; the rest show the limited realism of the carnally minded by forgetting to give this so much as a thought. These two approaches not only divide the converted from the unconverted: they are present as alternatives with every situation that meets the Christian.

Notes: V. 22: the wording of the references to Hebron in Genesis suggests that in Abraham's day it had not yet received its present name. V. 32: 'So they brought . . . ', rather, 'And they brought . . .'. I.e., they are now changing their tune from v. 27, regardless of inconsistency. To say that the land devoured (i.e. could not support) its inhabitants was incompatible with both the welcome evidence of the fruit and the unwelcome evidence of the giants. V. 33: the Nephilim occur only here and in Gen. **6**.4 (AV, 'giants').

Numbers 14 — The Great Refusal

The force of the time-note 'that night' (1)—since the spies had returned in daytime (cf. **13**.26c)—is that the night was deliberately given up to lamentation, with the inevitable result seen in the morbid fantasies of vs 2 f. (Paul and Silas knew better than to court this danger, Acts **16**.25.) Moses now had to listen to hysterical death-talk (2) such as he himself had indulged in (**11**.15); but theirs, unlike his, was defiant: note the ugly mood of v. 10.

The stability of the true servant, proof against fear or favour, is finely displayed here. In face of fear, all four who are named in vs. 5 f. (including Aaron, loyal again after his repentance in **12**.11) lean hard into the will of God. The prostration in v. 5 is to the Lord, in full view of ('before') the crowd, and the speech of Joshua and Caleb pivots on His purpose and calling (8). Tested next by the favour held out in v. 12b, Moses can rise above it through his overriding concern for his Master's good name (13 ff.), not his own. Here it is interesting to see the lasting impression evidently made on him, months before, at the 'cleft of the rock' (Exod. **33**.22), when he had learnt that God's glory resides in His goodness (Exod. **33**.18 f.; **34**.6 f.), for his prayer now regards the 'power' of the Lord as made 'great' (17) supremely in the exercise of His longsuffering (18 f.).

With God's startling proposition (12; see on Deut. **9**.14) compare John **6**.6: 'This He said to test him.' The test crystallized, and thereby strengthened, Moses' sturdy devotion; indeed the insight he displayed was itself God-given, as shown above.

Since God's mercy, however, is not laxity, as Moses had acknowledged (18b), the forgiveness of Israel (20) excluded the persistently impenitent (22; note 'ten times'). On this, we may observe that (*i*) their judgement granted them the fate they asked for; (*ii*) their children suffered, for a while, on their account (33, but 31); (*iii*) God's vision, unlike theirs, ranged far outside the immediate time and place: see the great prospect of v. 21.

The final episode, vs. 39 ff., strikes a note which is heard in many sayings in the Gospels: that second thoughts can come too late, and the opportunity be over. For the name Hormah (45) see on **21**.1–3.

Questions for further study and discussion on Numbers chs. 7—14

1. In the note on **11**.28 f. a comparison is drawn between Moses' reply to Joshua and Christ's reply to John. Besides the points noted in the N.T. specifically (e.g. 1 Cor. **10**.2; Heb. **3**.2), are there any illuminating comparisons and contrasts to be drawn between Moses and Christ? (E.g. Num. **11**.10–15 with Luke **9**.41?)
2. Note all that Moses said in reply to the criticism of him in ch. **12**. In 2 Cor. **12** and **13**, compare Paul under attack. Is there a common motive behind their divergent methods?
3. What lessons does the N.T. draw from Israel's great refusal in the wilderness? See especially Acts **7**; 1 Cor. **10**; Heb. **3** f.

5. FURTHER LAWS AND LAWLESSNESS: Numbers 15—19

Numbers 15 — Ritual Additions and Clarifications

Accompaniments to a sacrifice (1–12). It is here that we learn that the animal sacrifices of Lev. **1** and **3** must be accompanied by cereal food and wine, perhaps to make use of the conventions of hospitality to encourage and express a festive, ungrudging approach. In this spirit, Paul regarded his possible martyrdom as the libation that would crown the sacrifice (Phil. **2**.17; 2 Tim. **4**.6).

A foreigner's sacrifice (13–16). The rule that homeborn and alien stood, so to speak, on level ground before the altar, paved the way towards the total equality preached in the gospel (Gal. **3**.28). Note that this stranger is a sojourner, no casual visitor, and must be committed to God's covenant by circumcision (Exod. **12**.48 f., cf. Gal. 3.27). It is an equal sharing in the grace of God. For other aspects of a foreigner's equality before the law, see, e.g. Lev. **18**.26; **19**.34; Deut. **24**.14,17,20 ff.

The first for God (17–21). This offering was a yearly thanksgiving for a land and crops of one's own (19) after the necessary spoon feeding in the wilderness, cf. Josh. **5**.12. It celebrated a proper coming-of-age, not with arrogance but with thankfulness for the means of self-support, and recognition of their Giver.

Lapses and defiant sins (22–36). The requirement of sacrifice for even unwitting sins (22–29) is a powerful lesson in holiness—as long as it does not reduce sacrifice to the status of a fine or a licence (cf. Amos **4**.4 f.). The severity of vs. 30 f. is the O.T.'s answer to this, and Psa. **51**.16 f. shows how it should be taken: to induce repentance, not despair. The right attitude to the two extremes of sin envisaged in this law is seen in Psa. **19**.12–14.

Verses 32–36, taken alone, might seem an example of an unwitting sin savagely punished, but vs. 30 f. supply the context and the offender's motive. It is this that can turn the most trivial gesture into a fundamental challenge. Note that the matter was not dealt with in hot blood (34).

Tassels (37–41). It was this part of Christ's garment that the woman of Matt. **9**.20 touched, and this that the Pharisees liked to enlarge (Matt. **23**.5). Some writers have held that in view of v. 32, with v. 39b, the blue cord was to bring heaven to mind even as one looked earthward. A Jewish calculation finds in the numerical value of 'tassel' in Hebrew, plus the customary number of knots and threads, a reminder of the 613 precepts of the Law. Dare one suggest, however, that this fashion of the time was adapted to serve a memory-helping purpose no more mysterious than that of a knot in a handkerchief? (cf. v. 39).

Numbers 16 — The Rebellion of Korah

This classic revolt (Jude 11) was the most determined challenge of all, with its coalition of sacred and secular leaders (1), its canvassing of prominent names (2b), and its broad front of attack (3, 13 f.). This breadth was in fact a weakness, since the credibility of the claim to universal holiness ('every one of them', 3) was hardly enhanced by the frankly material values of vs. 13 f. Probably there was a genuine difference between the two groups, the one actuated by envy (cf. vs. 9 f.), the other by greed (13 f.); the former group too small-minded to realize that their quarrel was with God (11, for they agreed to the test, 16–19), and the latter group too shortsighted to distinguish their gaol from their goal. It was now Egypt, not Canaan, that flowed for them with milk and honey (13).

With a lesser man than Moses, v. 4 would have read, '. . . he drew himself up'. It is the man of small moral stature (it has been said) who must stand on his dignity. Moses, here and elsewhere, is sufficiently the servant of God (see on **12**.3 and **14**.5) to be master of himself and to submit the whole question to heaven (5). Even his angry rebuttal in v. 15 is a plea to his judge, not a counterblast of abuse.

The genuineness of this stance was proved by the intercession of both Moses and Aaron for their enemies, twice over (22,44–48). The second of these is a striking action-picture of the strict meaning of intercession, i.e. interposing on another's behalf. Cf. especially v. 48 and Isa. **53**.12; **59**.16.

Note: Korah's picked men, the 250 who tested their claims with incense, were destroyed by fire (35 ff., cf. vs. 6 f.), whereas evidently Korah himself (see ch. **26**.10), his accomplices, and all who stood with them (27), were engulfed (31–33). But the fact that Korah's sons escaped (cf. **26**.11), to the lasting benefit of Israel (cf. 1 Chron. **6**.22 ff., esp. v. 28; see also the headings of Pss. **42**,**84**, etc.), shows that the warning of v. 26 gave an equal opportunity to all.

* Numbers 17 — The Sign of Aaron's Rod

The demonstration with the rods, which were the leaders' tokens of office (for this reason the Hebrew for 'tribe' is 'rod'), supplied a sign that was not only visible but lasting. A comparison of v. 10 with Heb. **9**.4 suggests that initially Aaron's rod (with the jar of manna mentioned in Exod. **16**.32–34) was placed in front of the ark (perhaps outside the veil, where it could be seen), but later deposited inside it. By the time of Solomon, however, the only remaining contents of the ark were the stone tablets of the Decalogue (1 Kings **8**.9).

The antecedents and the sequel of this incident are both instructive. Aaron's rod had already authenticated its owner's call, to any unprejudiced enquirer, by its part in the deliverance from Egypt: see, e.g. Exod. **7**.9 ff., 15 ff. This was conveniently forgotten. And the present sign, for all its kindly implications of supernatural promise and fulfilment (8, cf. Jer. **1**.11 f.), was the excuse to divert popular resentment from Aaron to the God who had confirmed His choice of him (12 f.). The clearer the sign, and the surer the appointed mediation, the deeper was the wound to pride. There is hardly a plainer justification than this for the N.T.'s distrust of signs as solvents of scepticism: cf. Luke **11**.29 ff.; **16**.30 f.; 1 Cor. **1**.22 ff.

* Numbers 18

Priests' and Levites' Responsibilities and Rewards

Access to holy things (1–7). The meaning of 'bear iniquity' in v. 1 is virtually 'be held responsible'; its implications vary with its contexts (cf., e.g. Exod. **28**.38; Lev. **5**.17; **10**.17; **16**.22). Here the setting emphasizes the perils that surround the realm of holiness: see chs. **16,17**; especially **17**.12 f. The gulf between laymen and Levites, which the rebels denied in **16**.3, and between Levites and priests (**16**.5–11), is now precisely defined, and the divine initiative in this arrangement is reiterated in the words 'gift', 'given', etc. (6 f., cf. **8**.14–19).

Priestly perquisites (8–20). The emoluments were ample, and their quality first-class (12); at the same time there were reminders that God's service has its high demands. Some of the meals were sacramental, eaten ceremonially as though on God's behalf, in token of His acceptance of the sacrifice (9 f.; see on Lev. **10**.12–20); others, while more domestic (11,19), were still hedged about with certain formalities (11c,18). Above all, the ban on landed property (20) was a test of where one's treasure was (see comment on **35**.1–8). The behaviour of the sons of Eli was to show, one day, how contemptuously a covetous priest could regard his dues (1 Sam. **2**.12–17). On the phrase 'a covenant of salt' (19), see on Lev. **2**.13.

The tithe for the Levites (21–24). On the antiquity of the tithe see on Lev. **27**.30–33. But like all matters of obedience, its observance fluctuated with the nation's piety. Both Malachi (**3**.8–10) and Nehemiah (**13**.10–12) had to rouse their contemporaries to take it seriously enough to support the Levites.

The Levites' tithe for the priests (25–32). This 'tithe of the tithe' (26) has an interesting bearing on the antiquity of the Law (cf. Y. Kaufmann, *The Religion of Israel*, pp. 191 ff.), in that a tithe from the numerous Levites of Moses' day would easily support the priests; whereas the proportions were reversed after the Exile, when few Levites returned to Jerusalem. The fact that this law, an embarrassment after the Exile, remained intact, to the detriment of the priests, is good evidence that the books of Moses were already regarded as unalterable at that date.

Numbers 19

The Ashes of a Heifer

This provision for ritual cleansing is the subject of a 'how-much-more' comparison in Heb. **9**.13 f., showing that the old institutions were 'a copy and shadow' (Heb. **8**.5) of the realities of the N.T., which surpass them at two points in particular: the intrinsic value of the sacrifice and the inwardness of the cleansing. At both these points this chapter cries out for fulfilment, by its tantalizing inadequacy as much as by its clarity of symbolism. The inadequacy is not only that of the victim (almost the proverbial sacred cow!), but of the tediously slow cleansing (12,19) and the wholly external realm in which it operated.The conscience, as Heb. **9.**9,13 f. points out, was untouched. At the same time the symbolism is all too plain in its emphasis on man's predicament, barred from God by the presence of death (11 ff., 14 ff.) which is part of his world, and isolated from his fellows by the contagion of his defilement (22). (The prophet Haggai was to use this regulation as a parable of the spreading taint of a single matter of persistent disobedience [Hag. **2.**10–14].)

This negative aspect is balanced, to be sure, by the varied symbols of atonement, in which nothing is spared to make the sacrifice as complete as it can be (see on Lev. **14.**4 for the cedarwood, etc.). The pains that were taken over this were a pledge of God's concern, but a pledge is no permanent resting place. Taught by such a chapter as this we can share the relief with which the gospel was intended to be greeted, as it swept away the need to pick a cautious path through largely unavoidable hazards, and enabled sinners to 'draw near . . . in full assurance of faith, with . . . hearts sprinkled clean from an evil conscience' (Heb. **10.**22), set free to attend to matters of substance, unmixed with those of shadow.

6. FINAL JOURNEYS AND ENCOUNTERS: Numbers 20—33.49

Numbers 20 — The End of an Era

The smiting of the rock (1–13). Moses, recalling this fatal episode in Deut. **3.**26, put the blame of his sin on Israel, and this aspect of the matter is endorsed in Psa. **106.**32 f. Yet it remained his sin and Aaron's; and its seriousness lay not in any technicality (such as the spoiling of the type of the once-smitten Christ) but in the fact and effects of unbelief (12). It is a surprising diagnosis, since Moses and Aaron seemed to show more anger than doubt—though there is a hint of the latter in the emphasis laid (in the Hebrew) on the phrase 'out of this rock?'. But their unbelief went deeper than any doubt of God's power; fundamentally it was a distrust of His attitude. Like Jonah, they were in no mood for mercy, whatever God might say. So they misrepresented Him, and His name was not 'sanctified' (12). An ambassador can hardly do worse by his sovereign. (*Note:* Meribah ['strife', 13] was also the secondary name of the scene of an earlier conflict [Exod. **17.7**]. Both are recalled in Psa. **95.8**.)

Edom's intransigence (14–21). The generosity of Esau (Gen. **33.4**) was not copied by his descendants, whose hatred of Israel, not without provocation (1 Kings **11.**15), grew more and more implacable: cf., e.g. Obad. 10–14. On the 'King's Highway' (17) see *New Bible Dictionary*, p. 700, where it is pointed out that 'datable ruins' bear witness that the road passed through occupied territory at this time. Israel's avoidance of a clash (21) is worth noting; their battles were fought, in the ensuing campaigns, only by divine permission or command.

The death of Aaron (22–29). This was not only death but disappointment (24); it made clear at the outset the imperfection of human priesthood, which would never rise much higher than Aaron, and would sink at times disastrously lower. The priesthood's double weakness, of mortality and sin, is pointed out in Heb. **7.**23–28, in utter contrast to the priesthood of the 'Son who has been made perfect for ever', and who 'always lives to make intercession'.

Numbers 21 — Harsh Realities

A war of annihilation (1–3). In view of the distinction in Deut. **20.**10–18 between inhabitants of Canaan and enemies elsewhere, it is significant that it was a Canaanite community against which God accepted this vow. The name Hormah (3) is related to the verb 'utterly destroy' (2 f.), a term used by Israelites and non-Israelites to imply a war that is also a kind of crusade.

The brazen serpent (4–9). The epithet 'fiery' (6) is enigmatic; it may have arisen from the painfulness of the wounds. The people's rapid change from abuse to entreaty (7) is reminiscent of Pharaoh himself; expediency was all. In such a context the patience of Moses (7c) and the mercy of God stand out in their true colours as 'love to the loveless shown'. At the same time, the remedy, free as it was, was for the individual to accept, by an act of trust as feasible as it was decisive. Our Lord used this incident, with its presentation of God's judgement (8a) as the instrument of His salvation (8b), to picture Himself as crucified, and to expound the offer of life—but now eternal life—to the individual who trusts in Him (John **3.14** f.).

By a familiar process, the brazen serpent later became venerated as holy in its own right (2 Kings **18.**4), whereas its only significance had been functional.

The journey towards Pisgah (10–20). After the discouraging detour to avoid Edom (see on Deut. **2**) the route was now northward again, up the east side of the Dead Sea. The 'Book of the Wars of the Lord'

(14) is evidence of Israel's concern to preserve in writing even the well-remembered songs of its great occasions (cf. Josh. **10.13**; 2 Sam. **1.**18). The snatches of song in vs. 14 f., 27 ff. may have served the same kind of purpose (but in terms of boundaries) as our 'thirty days hath September . . .'. Perhaps the verse in vs. 17 f. was a working song like a sea shanty; but its theme of water in the desert is evocative of more than physical resources (cf. John **4.**13 f.).

Victories over Sihon and Og (21–35). The kingdom of Sihon (21–32), destined for Reuben and Gad, was a stretch of Transjordan from the gorge of the Arnon (half-way up the Dead Sea's eastern shore) to that of the Jabbok, about 30 miles to the north. Bashan (33–35) was a rich pasture land still further north, in the region of the Sea of Galilee; half of Manasseh would settle there. So the eastern part of the inheritance was already won, and the first giant slain (Deut. **3.**11; Psa. **136.**17–22); no small token of victories to come.

Numbers 22 — The Hiring of Balaam

Israel's thrust to the north, described in ch. **21**, had now been followed by a return southward, still east of the Jordan, to the plain near the end of that river's course towards the Dead Sea. It was the final halting place before the invasion of Canaan. Here Moses would give his parting discourse (Deut. **1.**5) before ascending mount Nebo to die (Deut. **34.**1,5).

Midian (4,7), in temporary alliance with Moab, was a far-ranging desert people, whose hordes would be a scourge in Gideon's day (Judg. **6.**5), although one branch of them, the Kenites, had thrown in their lot with Israel (**10.**29 ff.; Judg. **1.**16).

For all his vacillation between good and evil—more accurately, because he rated money above either of them—Balaam is unequivocally condemned in Scripture (2 Pet. **2.**15; Jude 11; Rev. **2.**14, cf. Num. **31.**16). We may be surprised that God tossed him up and down as He did, forbidding the enterprise (12), allowing it (20), opposing it (22); mystifying him (23–30), chiding him for not seeing the invisible (32 f.); extracting his withdrawal yet refusing to accept it (34 f.). But He knew the man He was dealing with. Note the implications of the pious words of v. 19, in conjunction with v. 12: that to line Balaam's pocket God might be induced to reverse the destiny of a nation. It was clear enough in what sense he reckoned the Lord to be 'my God' (18). To such a man, the only thing stronger than the love of money was the fear of death, and these experiences were well calculated to produce it. Nothing that Balak could say would now move Balaam from the position of v. 38, try as he still would to serve both masters.

On the speaking ass, there seems as little need to fret about the mechanics of this as of any other miracle. It was as timely and purposeful as all Biblical signs: in this case a deflating reminder to the expert in visions and utterances that under God the very beast he rode could see what he himself was blind to (vs. 23,31), and prove a better prophet than he. Note that Balaam got the worst of the exchange not only with the angel (34) but—reduced as he was to a monosyllable (30c)!—with the ass. Cf. 2 Pet. **2**.16.

Numbers 23 — Balaam's First Two Oracles

The seven pairs of offerings (1,14,29), impressive as they might seem, were a caricature of true worship: a gesture to Yahweh at the shrine of a rival (Baal, **22**.41) or, later, at artfully selected places (13,27), using a sub-personal technique ('to look for omens', **24**.1) designed to circumvent or change His mind, not to advance His interests. All these devices were totally ineffective, as Balaam soon discovered (**24**.1). So far from manipulating God, he found himself speaking the potent words which gave effect to God's will.

(i) *A people apart* (7–10). Through Balaam's eyes, as he surveyed the myriads in this no-man's-land, came the impact of the truth (cf. 'What do you see?', Jer. **1**.11,13; Amos **8**.2), but the words were from God (5). Israel's special calling, and her recognition of it (cf., rightly, RSV's 'reckoning itself', v. 9), form a major theme of the Pentateuch, to persist throughout history. In alluding to 'the dust of Jacob' (10) God confirmed the ancient promise to Abraham (Gen. **13**.16; cf. **17**.5) in which the N.T. would discern the whole Church, Jew and Gentile alike (Rom. **4**.16 f.). On v. 10b, Matthew Henry made the famous comment that 'there are many who desire to die the death of the righteous, but do not endeavour to live the life of the righteous'.

(ii) *An invincible people* (18–24). Balak's attempt to change the oracle by controlling what the prophet could see of Israel (13) only provoked the classic statement of God's unchangeability (19) and an account of how *He*, not merely the prophet, saw His people (21). The translation of v. 21a is complicated by the fact that Hebrew often uses the same word for an act and its consequences; hence the RV has 'iniquity' and 'perverseness', where the RSV has 'misfortune' and 'trouble'. But the usage of the two Hebrew words rather supports the RSV's other translation of them in Hab. **1**.3 (an interesting echo of this verse) by 'wrongs' and 'trouble'. I.e., God saw Israel not as the wanton troublemakers that they were in Balak's eyes, but (21b) as His own army, triumphant agents of His own work (23b).

If the first vision, then, confirmed the promise to the patriarchs, the second emphasized the redemption from Egypt and the shattering conquests that lay just ahead for Israel. It was encouragement from a most unexpected quarter.

Numbers 24 — Balaam's Closing Oracles

Perhaps his own words, God-given, against the diviner's art (**23**.23) helped to wean Balaam from his omens (1), i.e. the superstitious study of random movements and patterns (cf. Ezek. **21**.21). He was beginning to glimpse the personal, purposeful rule of God.

(iii) *Israel in peace and war* (3–9). As the margin shows, the last word of v. 3 is obscure; and there are still more suggestions. But 'opened' is perhaps supported by later Hebrew and Aramaic. 'Closed' makes sense if it is part of a progress traced by the other verbs; but this is not very apparent, and it involves a slight change in the Hebrew pointing (as does the meaning 'perfect' or 'sound').

Israel's orderly array (2) conjures up to Balaam. a peaceful landscape, very different from the waste land where they are now encamped. It is a watery picture, one of those scenes where the spaciousness (6a, 'that stretch afar') and the informality (6b) of God's design blend happily with man's tidy cultivation ('gardens beside a river', 6) and busy contrivances (the 'buckets' for irrigation, 7). For any community, particularly the Church, this could be a parable of its best pattern, and a reminder that but for God's gifts, (cf. 'water' and 'seed', 7), all would be desert.

The warlike conclusion repeats much of **23**.22,24 to confront Balak again with the folly of resisting what God has miraculously begun. Once more this process is traced back beyond the Exodus (8) to the patriarchal call (9b; Gen. **12**.3). With the mention of Agag (7), so impressive then, so unimpressive now, the antiquity of the oracles suddenly obtrudes itself, to make Israel's continuity all the more striking. Agag was evidently a hereditary name or title for the Amalekite king (cf. Amalek's prestige in v. 20): the name reappears in 1 Sam. **15**.8 f., 32 f.

(iv) *Star and sceptre* (15–19). Balaam used no preliminary rituals now. He even showed some personal involvement and emotion (17a,23); yet the sequel proves that there was no repentance (**25**.2; **31**.16). The immediate horizon of vs. 17–19 seems to be the reign of David, as the list of conquests indicates. But in Jewish thought the 'star' was also messianic. Our Lord takes up this title, as 'the root and the offspring of David, the bright morning star' (Rev.

22.16). With the 'sceptre', compare Gen. **49**.10, a still earlier prophecy of David and, it would seem, of his greater Son.

(v) *Supplementary prophecies* (20–24). Balaam's vision travels beyond Saul and Amalek (1 Sam. **15**) to Assyria (Asshur) and its deportations (22), and on again to Assyria's own fall (24). Ships from Kittim (Cyprus) refer to Roman sea power in Dan. **11**.30, but hardly here, since Assyria had fallen long before Roman times. Even so, the range of Balaam's vision was immense.

Questions for further study and discussion on Numbers chs. 15—24

1. Starting with the references in the note on Num. **15**.13–16, supplemented if possible by others from a concordance, study the place given to the stranger and sojourner in Israel. Is there anything here to guide modern societies in their relations with alien minorities?
2. Some aspects of intercession are suggested in the comment on **16**.22,44–48. What further insight into its meaning and function can we gain from other parts of Scripture?
3. What can the Christian learn from the tithe laws, as given in Num. **18**.21 ff. and in Deut. **26**.12 ff.? Does the N.T. offer any guidance on the subject?
4. What warnings should we take from Balaam's acts and attitudes, and what lessons from God's handling of him?

Numbers 25 — Disaster at Peor

The Moabite's seduction of Israel was a deliberate stratagem after the failure of their original plan. It was Balaam himself (**31**.16) who conceived the idea—one that was sufficiently diabolical to be recognizable again in the tactics employed against the church in Rev. **2**.14, and indeed wherever a frontal assault is replaced by a policy of enticement. The N.T. dwells on both aspects of this affair: the spiritual disloyalty (Rev. **2**.14) and the physical lust (1 Cor. **10**.8)—or, in modern euphemisms, a new theology and a new morality. Note, too, the expression 'yoked' (3,5), which may have influenced the language of 2 Cor. **6**.14 (lit.).

By the conspicuous fate of the ringleaders, retribution had to be displayed before God as sufficiently meted out (4c). Such a background emphasizes the curse that rested on a hanged man (Deut. **21**.22 f.—but the word is different) as the visible object of God's judgement. Such was Christ for us (Gal. 3.13).

Verses 6–15. Retribution continues to be the theme, and atonement (13) is effected by an act of stark justice. It is the complement of **16**.46 ff., where the atoning act took the form of interposing the person and work of the priest between the wrongdoers and their due—an act which owed its efficacy to the real interposition to be made one day by Christ, vicariously judged.

On the detail of the number of victims given in v. 9 and the 23,000 mentioned in 1 Cor. **10**.8, L. Morris points out (Tyndale Commentary, *1 Corinthians*) that 'obviously both are round numbers, and in addition Paul may be making some allowance for those slain by the judges' (Num. **25**.5). On the divine 'jealousy' which dominates vs. 10–13, see on Lev. **17**. Note, too, that Zimri was no mere youth caught in an unguarded moment, but a man of standing (14) who flaunted his trophy before the whole penitent congregation (6). It was a cool and undisguised challenge, which Phinehas was wholly right (cf. Psa. **106**.30 f.) to accept.

Verses 16–18. Retribution remains the theme of the chapter to the end. This time it is corporate, but not merely nationalistic: Midian is treated as a source of apostasy, and the reprisal was to be Moses' last campaign (**31**.2). Note, too, that the Kenites, converts to Israel from Midian (**10**.29 ff.; Judg. **1**.16), were not penalized.

Numbers 26 — The Second Census

This is again a military census (2), like that of ch. **1**, expanded by the names of clans within the tribes (substantially those of Gen. **46** and Exod. **6**) and by a few comments. It is here that we learn of the escape of Korah's sons (11; see note at the end of ch. **16**).

The tribal figures vary unpredictably from those of the earlier census; e.g. Simeon (14) has dropped catastrophically, Manasseh and Ephraim have virtually exchanged totals (but perhaps their names should have come in their usual order) and other tribes have shown rapid growth or loss, leaving the grand total, however, very little altered. On conjectured interpretations of these figures, see on ch. **1**.

If this is unexciting reading, the occasion itself was notable. It was a prelude to action and a fulfilment of prophecy. The former of these is implied in vs. 52–56, where the tribal totals are related to the coming inheritance; and the latter is explicit in vs. 63–65, which make as good a summary of the book of Numbers as one could wish to find. The N.T. finds this a very live object-lesson for Christians: see 1 Cor. **10**.11; Heb. **3**.12—**4**.2.

Numbers 27 — Two Problems of Continuity

A test case of inheritance (1–11). Some other examples of the law's growth or clarification through new cases can be found in Lev.

24.10; Num. **9**.6–14; **15**.32 ff. On this occasion, as before, Moses showed a remarkable openmindedness—open, that is, to God (5), whose will he did not automatically equate with ancient custom. The five daughters, for their part, were admirable for their courage and spirit; and thanks to this constructive reaction on both sides to a problem which might have been nursed as a grievance, the whole incident publicly demonstrated God's approachability and care for individuals, far more vividly than an existing statute in the law book would have done. For us, too, it may have light to throw on God's purpose in subjecting us to situations in which we find ourselves deeply disturbed and temporarily baffled.

Joshua to succeed Moses (12–23). The long shadow of Moses' approaching death, an event which will not occur until he has given the discourse which occupies Deuteronomy, already points to the approaching era of conquest and settlement. Moses himself, to his credit, thinks of his people's need rather than his own disappointment, and so Joshua is commissioned, not in spite of him, but at his fervent request. It is the way God prefers to work: cf. Matt. **9**.38, in a passage which suggests that our Lord may have had the present incident in mind (cf. Matt. **9**.36 with our v. 17; but cf. primarily 1 Kings **22**.17).

By placing his hands on Joshua, Moses was openly commissioning him (18 f.) and sharing with him his authority (20). Deut. **34**.9 adds that through this act Joshua was 'full of the spirit of wisdom', although our v. 18 shows that already in some degree he possessed the Spirit (as his previous military and moral leadership bore witness). Together, the two passages indicate that he was freshly empowered for his new tasks in the act of being set apart for them (cf. 2 Tim. **1**.6 f.).

He must receive God's instructions, however, through the high priest (21), unlike Moses, to whom God spoke face to face (**12**.8). Henceforth the functions of leader and mediator of revelation would remain distinct until they were united again in Christ, God's Prophet, Priest and King.

Numbers 28 and 29 — The Calendar of Offerings

The companion to these chapters is Lev. **23**, which covers much the same ground but is not confined, as this passage is, to the sacrificial materials. The scheme here is to cover first, the daily, weekly and monthly statutory offerings (**28**.1–15), and then, to work through the calendar of feasts, etc., from Passover to Tabernacles (**28**.16—**29**.38), concluding with a note that the catalogue took no account of the more spontaneous occasions, and that it was faithfully communicated to the people by Moses (**29.**39 f.).

Two things emerge clearly from this formidable list. The first is the great importance attached to the regular continuity of worship, morning by morning, evening by evening, sabbath by sabbath, and month by month. Each of these must persist regardless of the extra demands of the others and of the festivals: see the recurrent phrase beginning with 'besides . . .', in **28.**10b,15b,24b, etc.; see also **29.**6a.

The second feature is the progress to a climax in the seventh month, whose events occupy the whole of ch. **29.** The festive beginning, with trumpets and a holiday (**29.**1); the solemnities of the Day of Atonement (**29.**7–11; cf. Lev. **16**); and the elaborate eight-day feast of Tabernacles (**29.**12–38), made it the crown of the year. But the sequence within those eight days is surprising, with the number of sacrificial bulls diminishing daily from thirteen to seven, and then abruptly down to one on 'the last day of the feast, the great day' (as John **7.**37 puts it). This decrease is so opposed to human ideas of climax that it is hard to resist the conclusion that the Author of these regulations shaped them to the pattern of the true consummation, in which sacrifice would cease.

Note, finally, that the liturgical year was linked to two symbols of onward movement, one recurrent and the other non-recurrent. The first was the march of the seasons from spring (Passover time) to autumn (cf. Exod. **23.**16). The second was the march of Israel from Egypt, through the wilderness (which the Booths or Tabernacles commemorated, Lev. **23.**43) towards the promised land. Both the O.T. and the N.T. see this as a miniature of God's scheme of human history (see opening comment on Lev. **23**) from the redemption of His people to the time when the world will know Him as King (Zech. **14.**16) and the harvest of the earth be reaped (Rev. **14.**15 f.).

Numbers 30 — Responsibility for Vows

The aim of this chapter was simply to state a person's obligation concerning the vows he undertook (2), and to clarify the position of those who were not wholly free agents: a daughter at home (3–5), a wife (6–8), and a widow or a divorced woman (9–15). The principle binding the father or husband was that he must own or disown such a vow once it came to his notice, without delay or vacillation. Silence gave consent.

To turn from this straightforward rule to the legislation in the Mishnah, and to the glimpses of contemporary attitudes which appear in the Gospels, is to be reminded of the uncertainties and quibbles which beset any law code (obliged to decide, e.g. what phrases just escape classification as vows) and of the cynical manipulations (Matt. **15**.5) and absurd values (Matt. **23**.16–22) which man's perversity imposed on such material.

Our Lord did more than indict the conscious hypocrite. His outright 'Do not swear at all' (Matt. **5**.33–37, cf. Jas. **5**.12), however, is evidently addressed to us as individuals in our personal dealings (along with the rest of the maxims of Matt. **5**), since the N.T. allows both angels (Rev. **10**.5) and men (2 Cor. **1**.23) to make affirmations by God when they are acting as His spokesmen. Indeed, God Himself, as Heb. **6**.13 ff. points out, used this means of confirming His promise. As to vows, Paul could use them with a clear conscience (Acts **18**.18; **21**.23–26), and while Scripture records some disastrous examples (e.g. Jephthah's and Herod's) it tells of others (e.g. Jacob's and Hannah's) that were highly fruitful.

What is always wrong, the 'evil' (Matt. **5**.37) that our Lord was concerned to stamp out, is the arrogance of arming our assertions or our prayers with a trump card of appeal or promise. A true character does not need the former, or a true faith the latter. Jesus and His brother James both point us to the sterling simplicity of a genuine Yes or No, which is worth exactly what the speaker is worth.

Numbers 31 — Vengeance against Midian

Abhorrent as this story must be, it is important to see it in its own terms. I.e., this avenging of Israel (2) was no private vendetta but 'the Lord's vengeance' (3) executed at His insistence, in face of at least a partial reluctance on Israel's part (14 f.) and as punishment for a specified outrage (16; see ch. **25**). The equivalent term to 'vengeance' in N.T. quotations is *ekdikēsis*, retribution, in which the idea of judicially giving a person his deserts is prominent. Note that Balaam now received the penultimate wages of sin (8, cf. v. 16, and comment on ch. **22**).

The character of the massacre as a cleansing operation was borne out by the quarantine requirements (19 f.) and the ritual use of fire and water (23; this verse incidentally throws light on the meaning of Luke 3.16). The mention of 'atonement' through handing over the portable spoil (50) shows that this act was a restitution of forbidden treasure (53), which had put the camp in jeopardy as Achan was to put it at Jericho (Josh. **7**.1). The roles of executioner and beneficiary, which go ill together, were to overlap only within the strictest limits.

The whole grim episode, with its imperfect agents, its dividends and its inclusion of the innocent with the guilty, is a microcosm of a creation that groans and travails, even though it is under providential rule (Rom. **8**.20,22). At the same time, its pattern of retribution foreshadows, however distortedly, the ultimate retribution of the Last Judgement, committed (John **5**.22; 2 Thess. **1**.7 f.) to hands which are wholly to be trusted and were first dedicated to salvation.

Numbers 32 — 'Do Not Take Us Across the Jordan'

It was common sense for Reuben and Gad to match together needs and resources: 'cattle' and 'a place for cattle' (1,4); but it was shallow to decide so much by reference to so little. They were fortunate in having to submit their case to the authorities (2) and be faced with other aspects of the matter. As always, a godly and frank observer could weigh up, better than they, their existing obligations (6), the effect of their example (7), the context of past events (8), and above all, the relation of their choice to their vocation (15). Since their impulsiveness and self-interest were all-too-human traits, the incident has a timeless relevance to decision-making of all kinds.

The revised proposal of vs. 16 ff. was a fine example of constructive response to criticism: neither tamely withdrawing nor obstinately persisting, but looking for a synthesis on the basis of what is right. The new plan required faith as well as courage, since the undefended cities, however well fortified, would invite immediate attack. The faith was well founded, and the happy outcome is recorded in Josh. **22**.

As for the later history of these tribes (who were joined by half Manasseh, headed by the clan of Machir: 33,39 ff.), their relative isolation became sometimes a temptation to aloofness (Judg. **5**.15b–17a, but 14b), and always a lure to their enemies (e.g. 1 Sam. **11**; Amos **1**.13; and cf. the place-names in Num. **32**.3 with those of Isa. **15**, an oracle against Moab). For all this, the eastern side of Jordan was an enrichment to Israel, for its beauty (Song of Sol. **4**.1), its balm (Jer. **8**.22), its fertility (Mic. **7**.14), and, not least, for the most famous of its sons, Elijah the Tishbite (1 Kings **17**.1; 2 Kings **1**.8), whose rural simplicity was to challenge the sophistication of the throne at a turning point in Israel's history.

Numbers 33.1–49 — The Log of the Journey

Concealed in this forbidding chapter, v. 2 is seldom encountered, but its importance is far-reaching, as evidence of not merely a natural concern to remember the Exodus events in substance, but a divine command to record them with precision. Other allusions to records written by Moses occur in Exod. **17**.14 (after the first battle); **24**.4–8; **34**.27 (covenant documents); Deut. **31**.9,24 (the law as expounded in Deuteronomy).

Forty stopping-places are named here (this excludes Rameses, the starting point), eleven of them belonging to the first three months' journey to Sinai (5–15). Two of the places in this section, Dophkah and Alush (13), are mentioned only here, and there are many more such in the rest of the chapter. It emerges, too, that the list is not exhaustive (unless it tacitly distinguishes between a bivouac for the night and a formal camp), since it names no stage-points for the three-day journey in v. 8, or for the 70 miles that separate Ezion-geber from Kadesh (36). It seems likely that the number of places transferred from Moses' log to this chapter was consciously limited to forty, a very appropriate total. Apart from the first and last years' movements (for the latter, see vs. 37–49 and the notes on **21**.10 ff.) scarcely any pattern can be reconstructed—which is again appropriate enough to the restless monotony of the years of wandering, though it is partly due to our inability to identify more than a few of the sites. With vs. 31 f. cf. Deut. **10**.6 f. and comment.

7. THE PROSPECT OF CANAAN: Numbers 33.50—36.13

Numbers 33.50—34.29 — Realistic Planning

Policy towards the Canaanites (**33**.50–56). It is again made clear that Canaan is to be not merely a national home for a refugee people, but a holy land. No fraternization, no mingling of religions (52), no scramble for the best places (54) must jeopardize this conception, which God takes with frightening seriousness (56). Notice, in passing, the combination of human planning and divine arbitration envisaged in v. 54, in that there was evidently to be a preliminary survey and division of the land into viable holdings of different sizes, and a classification of tribal strengths, before the specific apportionments were made by lot within this framework. The double-harness of hard thinking and prayerful submission is a permanently valid principle of decision-making.

The bounds of the land, and the territorial commissioners (ch. **34**). There is a similar list in Ezek. **47**.13–21. Israel came nearest to possessing the full extent of its inheritance in the reigns of David and Solomon, though the coastal strip remained in the hands of the Philistines and of Tyre and Sidon even then. Not all the places are known, but enough are identified to give a fairly clear outline, for which a Bible atlas can be consulted. As regards certain names: 'the Brook of Egypt' (5) is the Wady el Arish, about 100 miles east of the Egyptian border-fortresses. 'Mount Hor' (7) is obviously not the southern mountain of that name where Aaron was buried (**20.**22 ff.), but another in the north, so far unidentified. 'The entrance of Hamath' (8) should probably be rendered 'Lebo-Hamath', about 50 miles north of Damascus, near the source of the Orontes. 'The sea of Chinnereth' (11) is known in the Gospels as 'the lake of Gennesaret' (or of Galilee or Tiberias).

On vs. 13–15 see ch. **32.** Of the leaders in vs. 16–29. Caleb was the only survivor of the first generation, as was pointed out in **26.**65. His fellow survivor, Joshua, was already marked out for more than tribal leadership (**27.**18 ff.). Caleb, by his spiritual singlemindedness, was to prove as unflagging as men half his age: see especially Josh. **14.**10–14.

Numbers 35 — Special Cities

Cities for Levites (1–8). Although the Levites were not altogether landless (2 ff.), they had no continuous stretch of territory to call their own, and were probably never given their full rights in the 48 cities allotted them. They had to remind the authorities to make the allocation (Josh. **21.**1 ff.), and if Hebron and Shechem are any criterion (Josh. **21.**13,21) Levites were not noticeably dominant in the places they were supposed to own (cf. 2 Sam. **2—4**; Judg. **9**). Moses foresaw that having 'no portion or inheritance', they would share the insecurity of 'the sojourner, the fatherless and the widow' (Deut. **14.**29). The intention of the law, however, was that they should be posted throughout Israel as disseminators of God's truth (Deut. **33.**10), enjoying a modest security through their allotment of tithes, cities and glebe land (Num. **35.**3), yet dependent on God as their true inheritance (**18.**20). See further on chs. **8** and **18.**

Cities of refuge (9–34). These six cities, three on each side of the Jordan, are named in Josh. **20.**7 f. There is the true flavour of antiquity in 'the avenger (*gō'ēl*) of blood' and in the role of the congregation (12) and the elders of the offender's city (Deut. **19.**12). At Sinai God had promised to provide a refuge (Exod. **21.**13 f.), which would replace or supplement the altar which sufficed in the wilderness. Only in a city could the law for manslaughter be applied (25 ff.), or a refugee await trial (12) without the risk of starvation. Adonijah and Joab, who resorted to the altar (1 Kings **1.**50; **2.**28), were guilty of a different crime, that of treason, on which the king could make an immediate decision.

This law supplied a workable means of replacing blood-feuds by public justice, with proper rules of evidence (30) and tests to distinguish murder from manslaughter (16–24), changing the kinsman status from private avenger to agent of the court (Deut. **19.**12), who must settle an account for which otherwise God would hold the nation liable (Num. 35.33 f.). This penalty of death was laid down for mankind in general, not Israel alone, in Gen. 9.6. Cf. Rom. 13.4.

It is tempting to see typical significance in 'the death of the high priest' (25,28) releasing the manslayer. Perhaps Heb. 9.16 f., with its use of a non-sacrificial aspect of Christ's death, gives some encouragement to the idea. But what is taught unequivocally here is the sanctity of human life (cf. Gen. 9.6b), which made even accidental killing a serious enough matter to restrict the offender's liberty until the end of an era.

Numbers 36 — A Problem of Inheritance

It is instructive to see this fresh development in a matter that was raised and seemingly settled in 27.1–11. The new clause in the law was God-given like the rest ('according to the word of the Lord', 5), but each stage had first presented itself as a problem which gave cause for concern, and the present one arose out of an apparent clash of divine commands (2a,b,4). In such a case there must be a synthesis, because God's word is self-consistent. Here, the answer demanded faith and obedience, by limiting an heiress to marry only within her father's tribe (8). This was perhaps no great sacrifice, in an age less dominated by individualism than our own. But we can be grateful to this procession of sisters not only for enlivening these pages with their engaging names, but for providing one of the few contemporary examples of doing 'as the Lord commanded' (10), to end this book of selfwill and wasted years on a note of uncomplaining co-operation.

Questions for futher study and discussion on Numbers chs. 25—36

1. 'When a man vows . . ., he shall not break his word' (30.2). We know our Lord's teaching on this in Matt. 5.33 ff.; but what about simple promises? What guidance can we get, from Biblical events and pronouncements, as to when, if ever, a promise should be broken?
2. What view does the O.T. take of exterminations (by human agency, as in ch. 31, and by non-human as in ch. 16)? What exterminations (of these two kinds) does the N.T. mention, and how does its view of them compare with that of the O.T.?
3. 'Be sure your sin will find you out' (32.23). Find other sayings which present the sinner as a threatened or hunted man (e.g. Gen. 4.7; Psa. 140.11; . . .), and his punishment as something he has set in motion himself.

Deuteronomy

OUTLINE

THE PARTING CHARGE OF MOSES

1. THE PRELIMINARY RETROSPECT: chs. 1—4

2. THE COVENANT EXPOUNDED: chs. 5—26

A. THE BASIC PRINCIPLES: 5—11

5 'Face to face at the mountain'
6—11 'Him only shall you serve'

B. THE DETAILED REQUIREMENTS: 12—26

12 A Single Sanctuary
13 Penalties for Subversion
14 Laws on Mourning, Eating and Tithing
15 The Year of Release
16.1–17 The Three Great Feasts
16.18—17.20 Justice and True Worship
18 Priests, Levites, Charlatans, Prophets
19 Safeguards of Justice
20 The Wars of the Lord
21 The Restraint of Lawlessness
22—25 Miscellaneous Laws: Social, Sexual and Symbolic
26 'Flowing with milk and honey'

3. THE LAW PRESSED HOME TO ISRAEL: chs. 27, 28
27, 28 Blessing and Cursing, Inscription and Declamation

4. THE COVENANT'S CONTINUING CHALLENGE: chs. 29—31
29 'You stand this day before the Lord'
30 'Therefore choose life'
31 Changing Leadership, Unchanging Law

5. OUR HOPE FOR YEARS TO COME: chs. 32—34
32 The Song of Moses
33 The Blessing of the Tribes
34 The Death of Moses

THE PARTING CHARGE OF MOSES
1. THE PRELIMINARY RETROSPECT: Deuteronomy 1—4

Deuteronomy 1 — Recalling the Great Refusal

The geographical details of v. 1 cover a wide area, and are probably a digression arising out of the term 'the wilderness', to remind the reader of the journeyings which that word should bring to mind. The expression 'beyond the Jordan' (1,5) is more accurately rendered 'in the region of Jordan', since it can be used of either the near or the far side in relation to a speaker: cf. 1 Kings **4**.24 (=**5**.4, Heb.), Isa. **9**.1 (=**8**.23 Heb.).

There is a skilful selection of details throughout the chapter. The time note in v. 2 adds irony to that of v. 3a, an eloquent contrast between the achievable and the achieved! The allusion to the officers and judges (9–18) was equally to the point, being both heartening and challenging: it was proof of God's promise-keeping, by the reminder of what had wonderfully developed since Abraham (10; cf. Gen. **15**.5), and it faced the leaders again with the high responsibility they already shared with Moses. They would have no excuse for collapsing when he was taken from them (and the hard cases of v. 17b would still be catered for, as **17**.8 ff. was to point out). There was force, again, in characterizing the wilderness as 'great and terrible' (19 cf. **8**.15; **32**.10), since it highlighted the wonder of their safe conduct (cf. the vivid metaphors of vs. 31 ff.), the perversity of their fathers' refusal of the 'good land', and the disaster which a second rejection would invite.

Making itself heard through all the warnings and reproaches is the call to go forward in faith. As an object-lesson, Caleb and Joshua, at the forefront of the inheritors of the land, are contrasted with Moses, the last survivor of the disinherited (34–40). Moses, though he had also earned his own punishment (Num. **20**.12), stands here as head of his disobedient people, suffering on their account (37) though not in their stead (Exod. **32**.32 f.). This had been the price of their drawing back; but the price of pressing on unbidden had been just as high (41–46). Both warnings were relevant to the approaching campaign, in which, as always, courageous and obedient faith would be the condition of victory.

Deuteronomy 2 — The Wanderings and First Conquest

'The Red Sea' (1) here means its eastern horn, the Gulf of Aqabah, with the port of Elath or Ezion-geber (8) at its northern tip. For

Israel it had meant turning south, away from Canaan (cf. **1.40**), to pace out the course they had cravenly chosen for themselves, little as they liked it in the event (Num. **21.4**). In its truth to the logic of the situation it was a penalty typical of God's judgements.

Now, after 38 years of nomadism (3,14), the meandering had turned to a march; yet the theme of this chapter is the tight control of this movement by God's decrees. The theme is given extra depth by the 'asides' which show how others entered *their* inheritances by divine allotment (note especially 12b, cf. 5,9,19,21b–22). Any idea that to be the chosen people was to be a master race was ruled out as early as this. They had their allotted place in its appointed time (Gen. **15**.13–16), with no more absolute freehold than had their heathen predecessors (Lev. **18**.28; **25**.23). Amos would have to remind them of this forgotten lesson (Amos **3**.1 f.; **9**.7 ff.).

In contrast to the peoples of vs. 1–19, the Amorites (26–37) were ripe for judgement (Gen. **15**.16; see also comment on Deut. **3.6**), and God now enhanced their king's aggressiveness (30; cf. Num. **21**.26–30) to bring about his ruin (cf. Rom. **9**.17 f.). It was another aspect of divine judgement; cf. the first paragraph, above.

Notes: Some of the names of the early inhabitants in vs. 10–12, 20–23, occur also in Gen. **14**.5 f. Some are alternative names for the same people (11,20). For details, see the *New Bible Dictionary*. On v. 29, with its apparent disagreement with Num. **20**.21; Deut. **23**.3 f., a possible explanation is that not all the outlying settlements followed the hostile policy of their leaders, and Israel was glad to do business with such groups. (So G. T. Manley, *New Bible Commentary*.)

Deuteronomy 3 — The Retrospect Concluded

The policy of extermination (6), already used against Sihon (**2**.34 f.), was to be standard procedure against the peoples that Israel was to dispossess, but was not to be employed against any and every enemy. See **20**.10–15,16–18, where the reason for this discrimination is explained. God alone has the right to pronounce such a sentence (which is a special case of His universal sentence of mortality, Psa. **90**.5 ff.); and it is worth noting (*a*) that the first two exterminations in Scripture were independent of human agents and fallible motives (Gen. **6**.7; **19**.24 f.); (*b*) that the Canaanite massacres left room for a Rahab and her family, as the Genesis ones left room for Noah and Lot, with theirs; (*c*) that our Lord's advice is to treat reports of violence and tragedy chiefly as signs of a world under judgement, rather than as material for moralizing (Luke **13**.1–5;

17.26–37); (*d*) that final judgement will correct the approximations that are inevitable in temporal judgements (Luke **10.**12 ff.). See also on Num. **31**, throughout.

King Og (11), as the last of the giants (AV[KJV]), with his 13′ 6″×6′ 0″ iron bedstead, has had some translation queries raised about him. Was his iron bed perhaps a basalt sarcophagus, and can Rephaim mean 'giants'? But the familiar interpretation is probably right. A huge sarcophagus is an unlikely trophy to transport to another kingdom, and both 'iron' and 'bed' are common words. And Rephaim, though it is an elusive term, has associations with hugeness in **2.**10 f., 20 f., and was translated 'giant' in the Greek of Josh. **12.**4 and elsewhere.

On vs. 12–22, see on Num. **32.** Verses 23–29 faithfully reflect the tantalizing situation of Moses, which has already made itself felt in **1.**37 f. The former reference (where see comment) seems to belong to the beginning of the wanderings, where Moses himself was guiltless. The present one certainly belongs to the end (23), but even so, Moses' guilt was incurred under Israel's provocation (cf. v. 26 with Psa. **106.** 32 f.), and God's refusal was couched in terms that may well have comforted Moses by their striking resemblance to the great promise to Abram: cf. v. 27 with Gen. **13.**14.

Deuteronomy 4 'Therefore . . .'

The retrospect has covered grace and judgement: no promise, no warning, has failed. And all has been verifiable: 'Your eyes have seen . . .' (3). Yet its meaning can be missed or forgotten (9), so this chapter sees to it that history does not degenerate into reminiscence but makes its mark on belief and action.

'*The word*' (2) is the first emphasis: vs. 1–14. Its character as unalterable truth (2,9,13) and as a challenge to the will ('statutes . . . ordinances . . . commandments') made this a humbling revelation, but a steadying one to live by, independent as it was of fashions of thought, and manifestly superior to any existing system (6 f.).

The second emphasis is on *the invisible God*. The theme has arisen in connection with His self-disclosure through words: 'no form . . . only a voice' (12). It dominates vs. 15–31 with the reiterated warnings against idolatry and (19) against astral worship; warnings whose relevance subsequent history was to confirm. (The force of v. 19b is that the stars, etc., are objects created for the benefit of all, not powers controlling national destinies.) The implied seriousness of idolatry, which at first sight may seem as exaggerated to us as it did to them, was not primarily through its denial of truth (though this is exposed in v. 28) but through its breach of the covenant

(23 f.). Because this was a personal bond between the Lord and Israel, any flirtation with other gods or substitute-figures would be as radical a betrayal as adultery would be in a marriage. So idolatry, a marginal sin to human eyes, could only lead to national disaster (26).

The third emphasis is on God as *the only God* (32–40). From a simple comparison of Sinai and the Exodus with any events attributed to other gods, the passage builds up to the twin statements of absolute monotheism in vs. 35, 39,which are as emphatic as anything in Isa. **40** ff., where the doctrine is often said to be first encountered. Intertwined with such a theme, note the pattern of grace, e.g. in the sequence 'He loved . . . and chose . . . and brought you out . . . to bring you in, to give you . . .' (37 f.).

Verses 41–49 mark the transition from the preliminary discourse to the main speech of the book (chs. **5—26**). Verses 41–43(cf. Num. **35**.9 ff., esp. v. 14) round off the former, and vs. 44–49 look forward to the latter (note the terms of v. 45a ,which suit the material of chs. **5—26** better than that of chs. **1—4**). Verse 46a sets the scene; vs. 46b–49 digress to recall the initial conquests that were the pledge of the full inheritance.

2. THE COVENANT EXPOUNDED: Deuteronomy 5—26
A. THE BASIC PRINCIPLES: **5—11**.

Deuteronomy 5 — 'Face to Face at the Mountain'

It is important to relate the 'statutes and . . . ordinances' (1) to the bigger reality, the 'covenant' (2) whose ends they served—somewhat as the rules of a household serve but do not constitute the family or the marriage. Chapters **5—11** dwell on the covenant partnership itself, of God and Israel, partly by recollection, partly by instruction and appeal. It is settled at the outset that there are no merely derivative members, who must share in the covenant at second hand (2 f.). To the second generation as much as the first, the Sinai confrontation was to be reckoned their own, 'face to face' (4). It is an O.T. counterpart, in its sphere, of the 'once for all' and the 'today' of the gospel.

The ten commandments (**5**.6–22). On these ten 'words' (22, cf. **4**.13, lit.), see further on Exod. **20**. In **4**.13 they are equated with the covenant, since they were its title-deed or 'marriage-lines', for which the 'ark of the covenant' might be called the deed-box. The opening phrase (6a) expresses God's side of the mutual self-giving which is the essence of a covenant, and vs. 7–15 spell out man's side of it—somewhat as a marriage vow specifies the love, honour and obedience implied in the bride's response. The 'manward' commandments

(16–21) continue the same theme, for they are the acid test of our Godward profession (cf., e.g. Jer. **7**.9 f.). The slight variations from the Exod. **20** version (chiefly v. 15's mention of Egyptian bondage, instead of the Creator's rest, to encourage sabbath keeping; also a smaller change in v. 21) suggest a preacher's greater degree of freedom than a reader's; perhaps, too, they point to a structure consisting of a brief command (e.g. 'You shall not covet') followed by a more flexible expansion.

The overwhelming presence (**5**.23–33). This vivid memory of Sinai is a significant prelude to the law, especially the ritual law, revealing as it does the unbearable impact of holiness on the sinner. It was a standing reminder that the law's elaborate screen between God and the worshipper was no show of aloofness but a necessity, begged for by man himself. Ponder the contrast, by grace, between Rev. **6**.16 and Rev. **22**.4.

Deuteronomy 6 — The Heart of the Matter

Verses 4 f., known as the *Shema* ('Hear . . .'), were picked out as the primary commandment, not only by our Lord, but by others of His day (Luke **10**.25 ff.) and by traditional Judaism. It is part creed, part command; and the warmth of the latter flows rightly from the personal emphasis of the former, with its reiterated name 'Yahweh . . . one Yahweh' and its echo of the covenant in speaking of '*our* God'. This is a monotheism that is reached, not by elimination of other hypotheses, but by revelation, explicit and by name, with grace at its heart in the self-giving implied in His commitment to His people.

'You shall love . . .' (5) is the only motivation that makes Law fruitful, for God's commands are given to define how love must show itself in different contexts, not how little one can get away with, or how much merit one can acquire. 'Heart and soul' denote the whole range of one's being, and 'might' denotes the intensity (cf. Eccl. **9**.10—but a different word) of one's loving. The addition of 'mind' in the N.T. quotations only makes explicit what is implied in 'heart' in the O.T., which includes both mind and will. 'Soul' is almost synonymous with 'self'. For the three words together, see 2 Kings **23**.25.

The people of a book (6–9). As against most religions, which inculcate routines, God looks for knowledge and understanding (cf. also v. 20), and sees the home and the common round as its school. As against the modern fear of overdoing matters, He requires His teachings to be the very stuff and pattern of a family's life (7); as gladly worn as a ring or an ornament; as obvious as their front door (8 f., cf. **11**.18–20). (It was a mistaken literalism that invented phylacteries [text-cases worn on the arm and forehead], as a comparison with Exod. **13**.9,16; Prov. **3**.3, indicates.)

'*That it may go well with you*' (3,18, cf. 24). This is a constant theme of Deuteronomy, which marries the idea of absolute obligation (e.g. vs. 1,13,25) with that of finding fulfilment in life. In human systems of ethics these tend to be alternative rather than complementary criteria; it is God's total authority and perfect love which bring them together. Cf. the two halves of v. 24, where this harmony is perfectly expressed.

Deuteronomy 7 — Israel and the Gentiles

(i) '*No covenant . . ., no mercy*' (1–5). For the identities of the 'seven nations' (1), as far as they are known at present, see a reference book, e.g. the *New Bible Dictionary*. On the word for 'utterly destroy' (2), see on Num. **21**.1–3. Cf. vs. 25 f. here, where 'accursed thing' (*ḥērem*) is the corresponding noun. The 'pillars' and 'Asherim' (not 'groves', AV [KJV]) of v. 5 appear to have been stone and wooden representations of, respectively, a god (El or Baal?) and the principal Canaanite goddess Asherah.

(ii) '*Chosen*' (6–11). This key paragraph on the choice, or 'election', of Israel gives no encouragement to the complacency, pride or speculation it might be expected to provoke. Complacency is forestalled by the emphasis on the end in view (to be 'holy' and to be 'His', 6, cf. the similar stress in Eph. **1**.4–6) and by the warning that they are to take no liberties (10 f.). Pride is punctured by the 'not because . . .' in v. 7 (cf. **9**.5 and the gospel's 'not because . . .' in, e.g. Tit. 3.5). And there is no room for speculation in face of the clause 'because the Lord loves you' (8), which puts the matter beyond argument—unless we think to judge divine love by human. The paragraph as a whole encourages humble confidence in the One who has begun and continued (8 f.) so surprising a thing.

(iii) '*Blessed above all peoples*' (12–16). Deuteronomy visualizes a people and country that will be the envy of the world. This eager anticipation, which keeps breaking through, is strong evidence of the genuineness of its professed setting, looking in from the outside to a land of plenty, and ahead to great possibilities. The blessings of these verses will be elaborated in **28**.1–14.

(iv) '*You shall not be afraid of them*' (17–26). Whether the 'hornets' (20) were meant literally or symbolically (cf. Isa. 7.18), this was a reminder that fresh 'signs' and 'wonders' (19) would meet the new situation. But note the deliberate limitation decreed in v. 22, an important verse for interpreting the conquest summaries in Joshua (which are themselves balanced by, e.g. Josh. 13.1 ff.), and for understanding God's frequent choice of gradual or modest conquests in the spiritual war. He knows how much His people are ready to handle and consolidate.

Deuteronomy 8 'Facing either Poverty or Plenty'

The temptation of Christ has illuminated this passage for us through His complete acceptance of v. 3b, not as an irksome demand, but as the secret of life. His later saying, 'My food is to do the will of Him who sent Me . . .', bears out the abiding reality this had for Him. For Israel it was a lesson learnt grudgingly, if at all. In fact the two attitudes to miracles implied in vs. 3 f. reveal the extraordinary insensitivity of sinful man to God, even when His power is on display. The manna was as unwelcome as a new coinage or a new hymn tune ('which you did not know, nor did your fathers know'!), and the sustained miracle of v. 4 seems to have aroused no particular gratitude. It was not proof that was lacking, but willingness to be convinced.

With relative affluence ahead (7 ff.) God's praise could be sung in a new key (10), but temptation would also take a new form (11 ff.). Yet it was still, at bottom, pride that was the snare: not the pride that objects to being 'pushed around', as in vs. 2 ff., but the unconscious complacency of the prosperous.

With regard to the 'iron' and 'copper' of v. 9, it was a happy irony that the chief source of these would be found in the Arabah, the tract of country between the Dead Sea and the eastern tip of the Red Sea (see on ch. 2), which was part of the 'great and terrible wilderness' (15). The most bitterly resented phase of the wanderings (Num. 21.4 ff.) had in fact traversed a region which would help to make Solomon's fortune. Some of God's best gifts to Israel (as to us) were those that were least inviting and least immediate.

Questions for further study and discussion on Deuteronomy chs. 1—8

1. 'No form; . . . only a voice' (4.12). What were the main reasons for the O.T.'s emphasis on this point, and for Israel's reluctance to accept it? In what ways is it still a live issue?
2. The N.T. quotes the last six commandments several times, but not the first four (5.6–15). Is this because it covers their subject-matter more searchingly? Study the N.T. teaching on these four areas.
3. 'What is the meaning . . . ?' (6.20). Has the answer to this question anything to teach us about explaining our faith to an enquirer? Examine what it says, and how it puts it.

4. **Show how Gen. 3, by its account of man's negative choice and its cost, helps to illuminate Deut. 8.3b. What example would you choose to illustrate it positively?**

Deuteronomy 9 — 'You are a Stubborn People'

This chapter is an important companion to the statement in 7.6 ff. on God's choice of Israel. There, they were reminded of their political insignificance; here, of their moral unworthiness (4 f.), which the rest of the chapter expounds as essentially that of their mutinous spirit. Not the sins of weakness but those of defiance are picked out here, with the Golden Calf as the most revealing example—man's outrageous footnote to the deed of union with his Maker. The breaking of the tablets by Moses (17) incidentally makes their character fully clear as the certificate and summary of this covenant (cf. 11b), not as a detached statement of the moral law. His action dramatized the threat of annulment which God had pronounced in v. 14, a sober threat which would not have broken the promise to Abraham but would have channelled it now through this one descendant of his.

Since this part of Deuteronomy was specially in our Lord's mind in His forty days of fasting, it may be that the two fasts of Moses, as covenant mediator (8) and as intercessor for a rebellious people (18,25 ff.), formed the background of His own thinking at this time. Certainly, Israel was in no less perilous a state then than in Moses' day.

As a matter of narrative technique, note the tendency to stress a subject more than a time-sequence. E.g., v. 11 adds the note of time after v. 10 has dwelt on the detail of what was given and received. Similarly, vs. 18–20 hasten to tell of the intercession, before v. 21 fills in an earlier detail (The RSV's 'Then', in v. 21, is unjustifiable; it is a circumstantial clause, i.e. 'As for the sinful thing . . .'), and vs. 22–24 pile up further sins of Israel before v. 25 picks up the threads of v. 18 again with greater fullness. This freedom to follow up a theme while the narrative pauses, or to jump ahead and return later for the missing pieces, allows the story to make its own emphases. (A classic example of the technique is in Ezra 4, where the modern reader must enclose vs. 6–23 in brackets, or lose his way entirely.) It is not hard to see where Moses wished his emphasis to fall.

Deuteronomy 10 — Divine Patience

Concluding retrospects (1–11). We can be grateful for Moses' first-person account of the new covenant-tablets, since v. 4 clears up the ambiguity of Exod. **34**.28, to show that the Lord Himself inscribed them. In v. 3 the meaning may be that Moses made a chest which served until Bezalel's permanent ark was ready (Exod. **37**.1–9; cf. **40**.20), but it is more probably another example of an anticipatory detail and a delegated task (see the final comment on ch. **9** above).

The parenthesis of vs. 6 f. seems to be editorial, being in the third person—perhaps an extract from the same 'log' that Num. **33** drew upon (see comments there), v. 6 telling of a return over the same ground as Num. **33**.31. The death of Aaron is brought to mind, no doubt, through the recollection of Sinai (cf. **9**.20). In vs. 8 f. Moses is again the speaker (notice the personal touch, '*your* God'), and Sinai/Horeb is the scene, the time-note in v. 8a referring to Exod. **32**.26–29 completed by Num. **3**.14 ff. So the bracket in the RV/RSV should be closed after v. 7, not after v. 9. Moses' thought has again reverted to the crisis at the foot of Sinai and to the great intercession, which he recounts for the third time: vs. 10 f., cf. **9**.18,25.

The only right response (12–22). With the purposeful 'And now—' (a common expression in letters of O.T. times, to introduce the main topic), Moses sums up the issue before Israel, in an appeal which will reach its climax in the last paragraph of ch. **11**. In terms of treaty-making, the customary preamble and historical survey, already heard, are now followed by the 'declaration of basic principle' (von Rad), before the detailed stipulations of chs. **12—26**, and the clinching blessings and curses of chs. **27—28**.

Notice how many of the themes of the foregoing chapters are rapidly reviewed in vs. 12–22: the great commandment (12), the beneficent laws ('for your good', 13), the monotheistic faith (14), the election of Israel (15), etc., etc. It is a good exercise to search out the passages which speak again here.

Deuteronomy 11 The Only Right Response (concluded)

A loving obedience, which nevertheless takes no liberties with God, is the substance of this appeal. It is put quite directly in the exhortations of, e.g. vs. 1,13, 22,and in the frank reminders of the first and last paragraphs, but it also comes through, indirectly, in the tone and spirit of the central sections. The speaker's delight at Israel's prospect of living in direct dependence on heaven (11), after the tame predictability of Egypt, that man-made kitchen-garden (10), is not the usual human attitude, which prefers a more controllable situation. To the self-willed, the promise of v. 12 is an intrusion, and the warning of vs. 16 f. an example of unfair pressure; but

Moses speaks as a lover of God, and calls his hearers to the same commitment.

So there is no middle way contemplated. For each household the goal is total exposure to the word of God (vs. 18–20 repeat the striking demand of **6**.6–9 in very similar terms), and for the nation the choice between blessing and cursing must be dramatized as a deep divide (the two mountains, Gerizim and Ebal [29] rise about 3,000 feet on either side of Shechem). But if these demands are extreme, they are realistic. They are not only true to the sovereign rights of deity, and to the best interests of His people (cf., e.g. v. 9), but they are reinforced by the fact that Israel owes her past salvation (4 ff.) and future victory (23–25) entirely to God.

Note: The parenthesis in v. 2 leaves very little room for argument over the historical setting of Deuteronomy. To see the book (as some do) as the work of later preachers, speaking to their own age in the Mosaic tradition, is to make this negative either meaningless or insincere, for its plain words would convey the exact opposite of the truth.

B. THE DETAILED REQUIREMENTS: 12—26

Deuteronomy 12 — A Single Sanctuary

The multitudinous laws of the next fifteen chapters are unified by the central theme of right relationship with God. The point of the present chapter, reinforced in its opening and closing paragraphs against paganism (1–4,29–31), is that Yahweh is *One*, and His single place of worship is to proclaim the fact and keep it steadily before His people.

Notice the emphasis on His own choice of this place, a point made six times in the chapter, since human religion loves to multiply superstitions at hallowed spots, while God on the contrary elects to 'put His name and make His habitation' (5, cf. v. 11) at a focal point. 'Name' implies a well-defined self-disclosure, and 'habitation' a settled place among His people. Gilgal, Bethel and Shiloh were temporary centres, but the chosen place would not be named until Jerusalem became the site of the Temple (1 Kings **8**.16,29; **9**.3). This in turn was superseded when 'the Word became flesh and dwelt among us', and worship was freed from physical sanctuaries (John **1**.14; **4**.21,23).

The other emphasis is on joy (7,12,18), a characteristic note in Deuteronomy. Here it arises out of the twin facts of material blessings (peace, e.g. v. 10, and plenty) and the warmth of fellowship, divine and human. Note the recurrent phrase, 'before the

Lord' (7,12,18), and the inclusiveness of the hospitality in the same verses.

Critical study of the chapter has chiefly fastened on its practical changes of sacrificial law. Lev. **17.3** f. laid down that no animal suitable for sacrifice might be killed 'secularly', but Deut. **12.20** ff. looks forward to relaxing this. Ingenious minds have speculated that this new procedure was tailor-made for Josiah's reformation (cf. 2 Kings **23.8**, etc.); but it makes perfect sense in its own terms. It took little foresight to realize that what was suited to the encampment in the wilderness would no longer serve in the enlarged territory (20) that awaited Israel. The same concern for purity of worship motivates both chapters: see Lev. **17.7**; Deut. **12.13** f.

As for the need of such purity, v. 31 reminds us that this was—and remains—no doctrinaire concern. There is no limit to the deliberate cultivation of evil, once the light of God has been quenched. Man then grows to love, and even revere, 'everything which the Lord hates'.

Deuteronomy 13 — Enticement to Apostasy

Unlike many penal codes, which prescribed death for comparative trivialities, God's law kept it for major outrages against the human person and, as here, against the theocracy. Note in v. 5c one of the Biblical principles of punishment: a concern for the purity of society. This does not figure much in modern theories, which give most prominence to society's physical protection, to the criminals' reform and to deterring potential offenders. The last of these is the motive in v. 11; but underlying all three paragraphs is the implied concept of retribution. The penalty is exacted 'because' (5,10) the offender has done a specific thing which deserves it, and which is satisfactorily proved against him (14). Cf. Rom. **13.3** f. On execution by stoning, see on Lev. **20.2**.

The test of a prophet by his attitude to the Lord, regardless of his signs and wonders, was a live issue in the days of Jeremiah (Jer. **23.16–22**) and Ezekiel (Ezek. **13**), and will remain so to the end (Matt. **24.24**), for even Christians can be dazzled by the miraculous. Verses 1–5 take precedence over the further test of **18.22**, which applied to cases where the prophet's loyalty was harder to assess.

Note, finally, the witness of vs. 12–18 to the disinterested motive for the ritual destruction of heathen cities. Here, with the same sentence passed on an Israelite community, its character stands out as a duty that overrode all self-interest and natural compunction.

The value that God attaches to undivided, but not untested,

loyalty (3b,4) could hardly be more emphatically proclaimed—nor the difference between His valuation and, for the most part, ours. Cf., in the N.T., the unfashionable plea of 2 Cor. **6.14—7.1.**

* Deuteronomy 14 Laws on Mourning, Eating and Tithing

For the forbidden mourning customs (1 f.) see on Lev. **19.28**, and for the food laws (3–21) see on Lev. **11**, where the list is virtually identical, and on Exod. **34.**26 for v. 21c. But the opening words of our chapter (1a) give a new tone to these injunctions, making the kind of appeal which our Lord used in Matt. **5.**45 for His much higher demands. They are a landmark, too, in God's revelation, as S. R. Driver points out, in assuring the individual Israelite of the sonship which had hitherto been ascribed only to the people as a whole (cf. Exod. **4.**22).

In the tithe law (22–29) there are some differences from that of Num. **18**, for which more than one explanation has been suggested. One is that in Jewish tradition a second tithe was given, over and above that of Num. **18**, and that every third year this (or even a third tithe) provided a charitable local feast as in vs. 28 f. (see on Deut. **26.**12 [Septuagint]; cf. Tobit **1.**7 f.; Josephus, *Antiquities* IV. viii. 22). Alternatively, this law may have been given to supersede that of the wilderness period, adjusting the Levite's share to the more abundant produce of Canaan.

The principle of v. 29b is one of the constants of Scripture, expressed in some memorable sayings, e.g. Prov. **11.**24 f.; Isa. **58.**10 f.; Luke **6.**38; 2 Cor. **9.**6 ff. It is true often enough in the material realm; always in that of the spirit. It will be the theme of the next chapter.

* Deuteronomy 15 The Year of Release

The opening of the chapter is similar to **14.**28 f. in style and spirit, and the last words of **14.**29 become its refrain (**15.**10,18). It is an exercise in faith and charity, not in hard-headed economics, as vs. 7–11 make clear—although v. 18 precludes any pose of moral heroism. Nowhere is it clearer than here that law without love is self-defeating, for its best intentions can always provoke the worst of responses (cf. especially v. 9).

In the realm of debts and slavery an Israelite's preferential treatment (3,12) should be seen for what it claims to be, the kind of help one expects within the family ('his brother', 2,3,12). It is no unfairness to one's business acquaintances that one's dealings with them should be financially sound rather than emotionally motivated; cf. **23.**19 f.

The clash between v. 4a and v. 11a is more apparent than real; the former speaks of what will happen 'if only you will obey . . .' (5), and the latter of what is in fact foreseen. Cf. John **12**.8.

The law on slavery is either more explicit at one point than that of Exod. **21**.2 ff., in mentioning the release of a woman slave as well as of a man (12), or else it has been modified in the forty years' interval. The former is more probable, as the Exodus law was chiefly concerned with a slave's marriage before or after entering the household (Exod. **21**.3 f.), a point which plays no part here. But what is vital to the whole enterprise is generosity (cf. the first paragraph, above). For lack of substantial help (as in v. 13 f.), of fellow-feeling (15) or of goodwill (18), emancipation has sometimes turned out to be more devastating than slavery itself; it is characteristic of Deuteronomy to urge that this should not happen.

The firstlings for God (**15**.19–23). This reaffirms the law of Exod. **13**.2,11–16, given in the context of the deliverance of the firstborn. The point of v. 19b is that man must not take a first cut of what is God's. Is there an implied allusion to this in our Lord's use of an unused colt for His triumphal entry?

Deuteronomy 16.1–17 — The Three Great Feasts

(i) *Passover* (1–8). Certain changes have been introduced to bring out the distinction between the once-for-all deliverance from Egypt and the annual remembrance of it. Enough is retained to bring it vividly to mind (note the references to Egypt in vs. 1,3,6), but the daubing of the doorposts with blood, which was the high point of the first Passover, has been abolished: the threat to the firstborn is a thing of the past. Further, there is emphasis on 'the place which the Lord will choose' (2,6,7)—for Israel will have *arrived*. Their fathers had eaten the Passover scattered and enslaved: their sons would be free and united. (Our Lord endorsed a Jewish continuation of this line of development by eating the meal reclining; contrast John **13**.23 with Exod. **12**.11).

(ii) *Pentecost* (9–12); (iii) *Booths* (13–15). On the meaning of these feasts see on Lev. **23**.15 ff., and the last two paragraphs of the comment on Num. **28**,**29**. Here the characteristic concern of Moses' preaching is not so much with the externals of these occasions as with the spirit of them, warm with devotion to God and friendly care for people of all sorts (note the breadth of vs. 11,14). The 'booths' (13) are explained in Lev. **23**.42 f., and are seen in use in the lively description of Neh. **8**.14–18.

In the summary of the three feasts (16 f.) notice the emphasis on giving, as an essential part of worship (16b) and as a testimony to God's prior gifts (17). The principle of v. 17 is taken up by Paul in 1 Cor. **16**.2 as a guide to weekly offerings, not only thrice-yearly ones.

Deuteronomy 16.18—17.20 Justice and True Worship

The theme of 'Justice and only justice' (**16**.20) is interrupted in **16**.21—**17**.7 by an even greater concern of this book, namely 'Yahweh and only Yahweh'. This still speaks to us, particularly when the 'contributions' of other faiths are urged on us. God leaves no room 'beside' His altar: see **16**.21. And on the relevance of this to justice itself, see **12**.31 and comment.

The highest court (**17**.8–13). Hitherto, Moses himself had been the arbiter of hard cases (**1**.17); now his work was to pass to a judicial panel, whose composition seems intended to be both lay and priestly (9). This was how Jehoshaphat interpreted it, giving special jurisdiction to the chief priest in religious cases and to the lay governor in political ones (2 Chron. **19**.11). The high authority of their office (10–13) is upheld by Christ in Matt. **23**.2 f., and its equivalent in a non-Israelite context is expounded in Rom. **13**.1–7 and 1 Pet. **2**.13–17.

The office of a king (**17**.14–20). How prophetic a charge this was, subsequent events would show. So apt were the warnings of v. 17 to Solomon that some writers have been tempted to re-date them in a later age—forgetting that for any king, David included, wives and money meant status and power; also that the danger of choosing a foreign king (15) was an issue hardly worth raising once the monarchy was established, but an open possibility before that. As for the king's duty to copy the law (18*), there was a modified acknowledgement of it at the first king-making (1 Sam. **10**.25) and perhaps a formalized trace of this at subsequent accessions (cf. 2 Kings **11**.12), but there is no record of any king making his own copy and studying it daily. The whittling away of an absorbing activity for the whole person into a formal gesture on a public occasion is rather characteristic in human affairs.

Questions for further study and discussion on Deuteronomy chs. 9—17

1. Study Deut. **10**.12–22 along the lines suggested in the concluding comment on that section.
2. 'You shall rejoice' (**12**.7,12,18). How do the circumstances that

* The Septuagint, mistranslating 'copy' as 'second law' (*deuteronomion*), gave us here the word that has become the title of the book.

are shown here help to produce true joy? What other sources of it are mentioned in Scripture?

3. In 14.1, the motive for a high standard of behaviour is that 'you are sons of the Lord . . .'. Search out other motivations in Deuteronomy which argue from the past, present or future. Is there a place for each of these in Christian preaching?
4. Deuteronomy emphasizes 'Justice . . . justice' (16.20) as fervently as it emphasizes love. Is it true to say that justice is the primary form that love must take in public administration?

Deuteronomy 18 — Priests, Levites, Charlatans, Prophets

The support of priests and Levites (1–8). As this short passage has been something of a critical battlefield it calls for a few technical comments. (*i*) In v. 1a, the RSV adds the words 'that is', thereby creating the impression that all members of the tribe of Levi were priests. This is grammatically unnecessary (Deut. **17**.1 has the same Heb. construction to express first a small group and then a larger one). If an explanatory insertion is needed, 'and' (AV [KJV]) is fully justified and manufactures no discrepancies. (*ii*) The additional priestly right to the animal's cheeks and stomach may have been an innovation at this moment, or a confirmation of an unwritten practice. (*iii*) A *Levite's option* (6–8) to minister at the holy city (instead of, e.g. teaching in the country districts: cf. 2 Chron. **17**.9) is equated by some writers with the country priests' deportation to Jerusalem in Josiah's reformation (2 Kings **23**.8 f.)—which creates a gratuitous contradiction between Deut. **18**.7 and 2 Kings **23**.9. But it would be surprising if such a perverse equation produced no problems for those who make it!

Ritual murder and the occult (9–14). Child-sacrifice and spiritualism are placed side by side, not only here, but in Lev. **20**.1–9, where see comments. Those who would defend the one may need to ask themselves why God associated it with the other, and why He considered all magic black, from ritual murder down to fortune-telling, in the long list of 'abominable practices' here.

The coming prophet (15–22). Here is the positive gift for which the foregoing prohibition is meant to clear the way (like all God's prohibitions). Instead of dark hints from mediums and omens, Israel will have the explicit words (note the plural, vs. 18 f.) of God, open to verification (21 f.). The criterion given here, that of prediction fulfilled, needs however to be partnered by that of **13**.1–5 (see second paragraph of comment on ch. **13**). Peter and Stephen were to quote this prophecy in their proclamation of Christ (Acts **3**.22; **7**.37). For us, this passage also brings the reminder that Jesus not only lived out but spoke out God's truth. We are to take His every word as authoritative, as He Himself demanded (John **14**.10).

Deuteronomy 19 — Protection for the Vulnerable

Cities of refuge (1–13). Little needs to be added to the comments already made on this subject at Num. **35**. Moses adds here the practical provision of roads (3), and an illustration of the law of manslaughter (5). The 'three cities' of v. 2 were to be in Palestine proper, since three had already been appointed in Transjordan (**4**.41–43). The 'three other cities' (9) beyond these six were never appointed, as far as we know, because the ideal territory promised to Abraham 'from the river of Egypt to . . . the river Euphrates' (Gen. **15**.18) was never occupied. David subdued and took tribute from such an area, which Solomon inherited (1 Kings **4**.21), but it remained foreign and was soon lost. Verse 9 therefore expresses a proviso which is implied even in the most forthright of God's promises, for these are never made to relieve us of our obligations; only of our anxieties.

The landmark (14). This was basic enough to find mention in the ceremony of cursing in **27**.17 (15–26), and to be proverbial, not only in Israel, but beyond (Prov. **22**.28; Job **24**.2, cf. the Egyptian Amenemope, ch. vi). Land was one's livelihood, and that of one's posterity as well.

Laws of evidence (15–21). Not only capital charges, as **17**.6 might have suggested, but all (note threefold 'any', 15) must be properly attested. This left its mark even on the dubious trial of Jesus, where the lack of convergent evidence exposed the inadequacy of the case against Him. The two further clauses here, the provision for divine arbitration (17, cf. **17**.8 f.; see on Lev. **8**.8) and the merciless penalties for false witness (19,21; see also on Lev. **24**.17–22) were excellent safeguards against every contingency but one: a régime of corrupt priests or judges. So the law gave Jezebel no difficulty (1 Kings **21**.8–14), and Caiaphas little enough. This would have been no surprise to Moses, who had no illusions about officials (**16**.19), or about the coercive power of law (see on **15**.1 ff.). For his definition of the spirit in which alone the law can be truly kept, see again v. 9.

Deuteronomy 20 — The Wars of the Lord

Procedure before a battle (1–9). This is the exact opposite of a 'commonsense' approach, (*a*) in its appraisal of resources, rating the invisible above the visible (1,4); (*b*) in its concessions to the preoccupied and afraid (5–8); (*c*) in its sequence of events, whereby the commanders are picked last (9). Yet it is not irrational: the priorities are realistic, as history showed repeatedly from Joshua to 2 Chronicles.

The 'officers' of v. 5 were assistant administrators rather than military leaders (cf. v. 9). In Exod. **5**.14 the name is used for foremen, and in Deut. **1**.15 for local officials. The concessions which they proclaimed in vs. 5–8 were probably designed not only to relieve personal hardship but to ensure that those who fought were the totally committed. This was certainly the motive in v. 8; and if fear is infectious, so is frustration (5–7; cf. **28**.30). There is surely concern, too, for the wellbeing of society, for military values are not treated as paramount: there are others implied here to take priority over them.

Rules of war (10–20). As regards the distant cities, v. 11 is illustrated by the story of Gibeon in Josh. **9**. Evidently the harsh terms of v. 13 applied only to those who chose to fight on, as Elisha's indignant question in 2 Kings **6**.22 makes plain.

The distinction between cities far off and near (10–15,16–18) was not military but judicial: the nations of v. 17 were ripe for judgement, and a threat to morality (18). On the policy of extermination, see notes on ch. **3**, first paragraph.

Verses 19 f. give their witness, with vs. 5–7 above, against 'total war'. Though exceptions could be decreed by God (2 Kings **3**.19), this general rule for Israel introduced a restraint which, in von Rad's words, 'is probably unique in the history of the growth of a humane outlook in ancient times'.

Deuteronomy 21 — The Restraint of Lawlessness

The unknown murderer (1–9). Num. **35**.33 had already established that to leave a murderer alive was to make the nation a party to his crime. The present passage allows no shelter behind the fact of ignorance—nor does it provide a formal substitute for the murderer if he is known: hence the animal sacrifice must be accompanied by the vivid disclaimer of vs. 6–9. (Had Pilate heard of this ritual? More probably its own eloquence accounts for its use in both contexts.)

The woman captive (10–14). Given the fact of war, enforced marriages could be as constructive a sequel as any, if the vanquished were treated with love. The law was sensitive to the woman's plight, giving her time (13) to adjust to her situation unmolested, and protecting her afterwards from exploitation (14). The shaven head and pared nails (12) would seem to represent her farewell to her former existence (cf. Lev. **14**.8 ?), as she discarded, too, the humiliation of captivity (13a), to have them replaced by the new growth and garb of her life as an Israelite. All of this acted out the Biblical marital principles of mutual respect and commitment, encouraging the attitudes that would make for a true marriage, even though (cf. v. 14a) it could not compel them.

The unloved wife (15–17). The unhappy families of Genesis (see especially Gen. 37.3 f.) are a living comment on this law, which cuts back the evils of polygamy but has no illusions about the quality of its fruits. The strong Hebrew expression, 'loved and . . . disliked' (lit. 'hated'), is the equivalent of 'loved and unloved' or of 'one loved more than the other': cf., e.g. Luke **14.**26 with Matt. **10.**37.

The rebellious son (18–21). Cf. **13.**6–9, and comments on that chapter. Filial obedience (cf., e.g. Rom. **1.**30; 2 Tim. **3.**2), is the first test of a man's acceptance of higher grades of authority, on which all order and stability depend. But see Eph. **6.**4.

God's curse on the hanged (22 f.). As S. R. Driver points out, hanging in the O.T. seems to have been the sequel, more often than the method, of execution (note the sequence in vs. 22 f., as in Josh. **10.**26 f.; 1 Sam. **31.**8,10; but 2 Sam. **21.**9)—which emphasizes its purpose as an exposure to contempt and execration. This is the passage which Paul quotes to show that Christ hanging on the cross became 'for our sake an accursed thing' (Gal. **3.**13, NEB). See also on Num. **25.**4.

Deuteronomy 22

Miscellaneous Laws, Social, Sexual, and Symbolic

Chapters **22—25** contain a profusion of brief laws, some grouped round a common subject (as in vs. 13–30 here), but most of them unarranged. The kindliest and the most unsparing, the lightest and weightiest, are heaped together without apology, since all are from God, although the reader is not excused the task of judging their relative importance and their place in the scheme (cf. Matt. **23.**23). See the opening comments on Lev. **19.**

Verses 1–4,6–8 are good examples of the partnership of love and law. Love is the motive in each case, but law directs it into wise and practical forms—e.g. summoning us to active help instead of neutrality or passive sympathy (2–4), teaching us self-restraint and respect for life (6 f.), and laying upon us the duty of taking precautions for other people's safety (8).

Verse 5 arises out of the scriptural concern to guard the built-in distinctions of God's creation. It does not specify particular forms of dress for the two sexes; these will legitimately vary with time and place. What is condemned is the perverted misuse of current custom; and since this is 'an abomination to the Lord' we are to regard this law as permanent, and respect its wisdom. The N.T. is no less emphatic against all tampering with sexual distinctions (cf., e.g. Rom. **1**.26 f.; 1 Cor. **6**.9, AV[KJV], RV).

Verses 9–12, however, are laws whose symbolism served a temporary purpose, like that of the food laws, to educate Israel in the pursuit of purity. Cf. the comments on Lev. **19**.23 and (for v. 12) Num. **15**.37–41.

Laws on chastity (13–30). Although the sentence of death could be commuted or waived (cf. Matt. **1**.19; John **8**.7), the fact that most of these laws carried it shows the intensity of God's concern over pre-marital loss of virginity (13–21), adultery (22–24), rape (25–27), fornication (28 f.) and incest (30). Note that although marriage largely made amends for the fornication of vs. 28 f., it did not make full amends (29a), and the couple were required to stand by the lifelong obligations that were implied in the sexual act (29b). With this serious estimate of this kind of offence, cf. 1 Cor. **6**.13b–20.

Deuteronomy 23 — 'Closed are its Gates to Sin'

Membership of the assembly (1–8). These provisions should be read, not as rebuffs for the handicapped, but as stipulations designed to guard the Church of the O.T., and to express in vivid physical (1), social (2) and historical terms (3–8) its calling as a company of the redeemed, without blemish or reproach, a people apart and yet not a wholly closed community (cf. 'the tenth generation', 3; 'the third generation', 8). Verse 1 incidentally offered Israel protection against the influence of cruel contemporary practices (see also on **25**.11 f.), and the rare word for 'bastard' in v. 2 may mean the child of an incestuous marriage: a further discouragement, if so, of deliberate social decadence. Other passages show that the genuine seeker, whatever his condition or origin, was always admitted: cf. v. 1 with Isa. **56**.3–5 (see also on Lev. **21**), and cf. v. 3 with the unreserved welcome to Ruth the Moabitess. Such a welcome was by grace; such a law made grace visible.

Seemliness in the camp (9–14). Although hygiene was well served through the rule of vs. 12 f., holiness, not health, was the main concern. It is the same theme as in ch. **20**, where victory depends on 'the Lord . . . that goes with you' (**20**.4). The words of v. 14 are as pointedly relevant to the Church as to the armies of Israel.

The runaway slave (15 f.). This humane law is in striking contrast to other ancient codes, which fixed rewards for returning a slave, and penalties (even death: Hammurabi 16) for harbouring one.

Cultic immorality (17 f.). Business, religion and lust pulled together in the Canaanite cults, which hallowed cultic fornication as a fertility spell for the crops and cattle. 'Cult prostitute' is lit. 'holy woman' (17a) and 'holy man' (17b)—a pungent commentary on pagan thought. 'Dog' (18) is a contemptuous term for the male prostitute.

Usury (19 f.). Verse 20 shows that lending at interest is not intrinsically wrong, only inappropriate within the 'family'. Lev. **25**.35 f. indicates the context that is in mind: not a business venture seeking capital but a poor man seeking help, whose plight must not be your profit.

Vows (21–23). The note of caution found here reappears with a characteristic addition of verbal pepper in Eccles. **5**.4–6. Peter seems to echo the principle of v. 22 in his rebuke to Ananias in Acts **5**.4.

Hospitality and its abuse (24 f.). Another reminder of the relevance of love (here in the form of elementary courtesy) to every level of human relations.

Deuteronomy 24 — Firmness and Kindness

Divorce (1–4). The RSV corrects the translations of the AV(KJV), RV here, bringing to light the fact that the first 'if' launches a series of hypothetical events leading straight to the 'then' of v. 4. I.e., the concern of the passage is not to recommend divorce in certain situations (as in AV[KJV], RV) but to decree that if such a step is taken it must be irrevocable. It thereby protected a wife against being virtually lent to another man, and it discouraged hasty action. So, while permitting but not commanding an existing practice (as our Lord pointed out: Matt. **19**.7 f.) it brought that practice under better control and upheld the dignity of marriage. Jeremiah incidentally used this law in a heart-searching analogy throughout Jer. **3**.

'*A kindness in His justice* . . .' (5–22). There is perhaps no better demonstration than this chapter of the guiding concerns of God's law. Where it is precise and hard (concerning the divorcee, 4; or the kidnapper, 7; or quarantine, 8 f.; or non-transferable guilt, 16), it is no less beneficent than where it is strikingly generous. All the rulings are examples of true justice, in that they are matched to the actualities of the case, although some of these are matters that count for little in official human reckoning, e.g. the founding of a happy marriage (5), the self-respect of the man who begs a loan from you (10 f.), or the fact that a poor man 'sets his heart upon' getting his wages punctually (15). It is specially worth noting that by making these benefits a matter of law, not merely of exhortation, God secured them to their recipients as of right. He has always liked to turn His beggars into princes (1 Sam. **2**.8).

Note: Vs. 8 f.: The leprosy rules are found in Lev. **13** f. The allusion to Miriam (9) was presumably to emphasize that no exceptions could be made: not even for an exalted victim or intercessor, or to avert great inconvenience (Num. **12**.14 f.).

Deuteronomy 25 — Miscellaneous Laws

Forty stripes (1–3). Paul's five beatings with 'the forty lashes less one' (2 Cor. **11**.24) were controlled by this law; the custom of omitting one stroke had come in to protect the court—not the prisoner!—from the risk of miscounting. In this passage, however, the penalty must be regulated 'in proportion to his offence' (2, cf. Luke **12**.47 f.), and the offender's human dignity must be respected: note the wording of the important caveat of v. 3b, and cf. the similar concern in **24**.10 f.

The unmuzzled ox (4). Paul's use of this verse to prove the duty of the Church to pay its workers (1 Cor. **9**.8 ff.) is an important witness to the relevance of the Mosaic law above and beyond its immediate context. Enough is commanded elsewhere to uphold the literal meaning of such a rule as this (e.g. Exod. **23**.12; Deut. **22**.6 f., cf. Prov. **12**.10), but God's self-consistency forbids us to stop there: we must go on in our giving to accept His valuation of human beings as worth 'much more' to Him than His other creatures.

Levirate marriage (5–10). This institution, which owes its name to the Latin word *levir*, brother-in-law, demonstrates the primacy of the family in Israelite law, overriding personal inclination and convenience. It incidentally shows that physical descent was not everything; a family was not merely a genetic but a legal or spiritual entity, and its continuance did not depend on the single thread of heredity. Twice in our Lord's ancestry this provision came into effect: Gen. **38**; Ruth **4**.

Indecency (11 f.). A somewhat similar item is found in the Middle Assyrian Laws (A. 8). The Biblical law seems deliberately framed to ignore extenuating circumstances, and so to fix absolute limits to what is permissible in an emergency. A general implication is that *not* all is 'fair in love and war'; a particular one is that God insists on the privacy of the sexual organs, and (as **23**.1 confirms) abhors interference with them.

Commercial honesty (13–16). The law is realistic in banning, not merely the actual use of false weights and measures, but the possession of them (the reader can reflect on this principle and possible applications of it: cf. Rom. **13**.14b).

Amalek (17–19). As in **23**.3–6, the events of the wilderness are treated with special seriousness, as being a time of decision and destiny—a miniature of His whole drama of judgement and salvation, with life or death confronting each participant. Cf. the treatment of the Exodus theme in Isa. **40** ff. and in 1 Cor. **10** and Heb. **3** f.

Deuteronomy 26 — 'Flowing with Milk and Honey'

Firstfruits, and the story behind them (1–11). This is evidently the other half, the worshipper's part, of the 'Easter Day' ritual commanded in Lev. **23**.9–14 (where see comment). The prescribed 'response' (5) enlarged the worshipper's horizon far beyond the bounds of simple gratitude for the promise of another annual crop. The wonder of seedtime and harvest is overshadowed by the greater miracle, the rise of a populous nation from the most meagre beginnings (5), and the story of its peril, rescue and triumphant arrival in the promised land. This is the Biblical perspective, rejoicing in 'all the good which the Lord . . . has given' (11), but still more in the facts of vocation and redemption. In the phrase 'a wandering Aramaean' the reference is to Jacob, most of whose family ties were with Paddan-aram. 'Wandering' is not the equivalent of 'nomad', a man whose roaming is purposeful, but of a creature in jeopardy like the 'lost' sheep of Psa. **119**.176.

A declaration after the three-year tithe (12–15). (The Septuagint of v. 12 reads '. . . the second tithe you shall give to the Levites . . .', supporting, if it is reliable, a point discussed at **14**.22–29, above.) On the forbidden activities of v. 14, see on Lev. **21**, especially the second paragraph of comment. As for the prayer of v. 15, its position is significant, following the account of shared wealth and loyal obedience (12–14), since this is the scriptural sequence: e.g. 'Give, and it will be given to you' (Luke **6**.38); 'Honour the Lord with . . . the firstfruits . . .; then your barns will be filled with plenty' (Prov. **3**.9 f.). Examples of this principle, in matters spiritual as well as material, are found in every section of the Bible.

The peroration (16–19). The whole chapter has played its part in concluding the great exposition of the covenant, begun in ch. **5**, by turning its attention towards the crowning blessing, the promised land. Now comes the challenge to work out in detail (16) the implications of the mutual commitment which is the core of the covenant ('You have declared . . . and the Lord has declared . . .', 17 f.).

Note the stress on 'this day' (16,17,18), for the original covenant was not part of a dead past (5.3)—there is no such thing with God's deeds: Eccles. 3.14, cf. Luke 20.38—and therefore the new generation must be confronted with it afresh. See 27.9 f.; 29.1; and for the Christian, Heb. 3.13–15.

Questions for further study and discussion on Deuteronomy chs. 18—26

1. 'That same prophet shall die' (18.20). What kinds of offences attracted this penalty in Deuteronomy, and what purposes was it meant to serve (e.g. 19.13,20 . . .)?
2. 'You may not withhold your help' (22.3). Follow up this line of thought, to see how far it is taken in the O.T. (e.g. Exod. 23.4 f.; Prov. 24.11,12,17; 25.21; . . .) and in the N.T.
3. In the comment on 24.5–22 it is claimed that the 'precise and hard' enactments in that chapter are as beneficent as the obviously generous ones. Do the examples given there bear this out? If they do, can the same be said of the laws outside this chapter?
4. The scriptural sequence, 'Give and it will be given to you', is mentioned in the comment on 26.12–15 as one that can be illustrated from every section of the Bible, in matters spiritual as well as material. Is this so?

3. THE LAW PRESSED HOME TO ISRAEL: Deuteronomy 27,28

Deuteronomy 27

'. . . The Words of this Law very plainly'

Word and sacrament: monument and feast (1–8). In Moses' day it was common for an emperor to insist that his vassals should exhibit copies of his treaties with them, and have them regularly read in public. God decreed both these forms of reminder: the first, as here, being the display of the written law, clinched by a sacred meal, and the second being its public reading, as laid down in 31.10 ff. If this is one 'fingerprint' of the antiquity of the chapter, the command to build an altar on Mount Ebal (4), near Shechem, is another; for this strategic spot was well suited to celebrate an invasion, but was not destined to be the national sanctuary.

Back to the present (9 f.). Note the return to 'this day (9) . . . this day' (10); to counterbalance the emphasis of this chapter on the future, 'over the Jordan' (2,4,12). The covenant must not be a dream projected towards Canaan, any more than it must be a bare memory of Sinai (see on **26.16–19**), for salvation may be rooted in the past and crowned in the future, but its effective moment is 'now': cf. 2 Cor. **6.2**.

The ceremonial blessing and cursing (11–26). On the dramatic setting for this, see on **11.29**. The imperial treaties of this time were reinforced with curses for disobedience and blessings for obedience, as here. It is another feature that fits the period. Here, to be sure, only the curses are actually enumerated, but the disposing of the tribes on opposite hills, with their two roles broadly corresponding to their ancestors' high or low ranking (the disgraced Reuben, the handmaids' sons and the youngest son of Leah being assigned to the mount of cursing), confirms that the ceremony presented both alternatives. And this is true of the next chapter, where Moses returns to 'this day' (**28.1**) and his present audience. The twelve curses here give special emphasis to offences which tend to escape human justice (either through secrecy [15,17,18,24] or through judicial corruption [19,25]), and to those that strike at the roots of society by flouting authority human and divine (16,26), or sexual decency (20–23). These are still the points where national decadence tends to begin and grow.

Deuteronomy 28

'All These Blessings . . . All These Curses'

Important as were the procedures planned in ch. **27** for a future occasion, it was the present that was paramount and that kept breaking into Moses' discourse (27.1,9,10: 'this day'). Chapter **28.1** can be read straight on from those interjections, and treats the hearers of Moses as bound up with the Israel of every generation ('you . . . you . . . your . . . your').

It is perhaps the most eloquent and moving chapter in an unusually eloquent book. Its structure is simple, consisting basically of two matching paragraphs of blessing and cursing in almost identical terms (1–6,15–19), suited to the kind of antiphonal ceremony that was described in **27.12** ff., each of which is then expanded in a longer prophetic discourse (7–14,20–68).

The leading themes of Deuteronomy are prominent in the passages of blessing (prosperity, victory and [9 f.] vocation), and are used to add to the poignancy of the negative passages (e.g. vs. 47,48,63). The latter are built up with extraordinary skill, not only in surpassing one climax with another, but in varying the large-scale descriptions with intimate touches of terror and pathos—e.g. vs. 32,34,37, and notably vs. 65 ff.

Still more impressive, however, is the fact that some of the worst of these calamities are encountered again, not as prophecy, but as history: cf. especially vs. 37,53–57,65, with the harrowing testimony of Lam. **4**. On the relapse into savagery under siege, H. Butterfield's chapter on 'Human Nature in History' (*Christianity and History*, ch. **2**) is illuminating, especially in pointing out the part played by 'the orderings and arrangements of a healthy society' in concealing from us 'the volcano that lies in human nature', which can burst into activity all too easily when there is a serious enough shift in our circumstances.

4. THE COVENANT'S PERENNIAL CHALLENGE: Deuteronomy 29—31

Deuteronomy 29 — Covenant Renewal

This rededication of Israel to its bond of union with the Lord is the immediate purpose of Moses' farewell address, and the whole book therefore displays the pattern of a contemporary covenant ceremony, with its preamble and historical review (chs. **1—4**), its general and particular requirements (chs. **5—11**, **12—26**), its preservation in writing (**10**.1–5; **27**.1–8; **31**.24 f.), its periodic proclamation (**31**.10–13) and its reinforcement by curses and blessings (**27**.11—**28**.68). For God's covenant refuses to be relegated to the past (cf. **5**.2 f. and note); it binds the new generation, summoned to take the oath of allegiance ('the sworn covenant', 12), and it reaches forward and outward to 'him who is not here with us this day' (15). The last phrase may have been in mind when our Lord prayed 'not . . . for these only, but also for those who are to believe in Me through their word' (John **17**.20)—embracing the whole circle of the covenanted throughout time and space (John **17**.23), as present together to His view.

But there is no glossing over the immediate situation, in which Israel is as dense and disobedient as, one day, Isaiah would find her, and as she would still be in the gospel age (cf. v. 4 with Isa. **6**.9 f. and its quotation by Jesus and Paul in Matt. **13**.14 f. and Acts **28**.26 f.). The reason for this is stated both in terms of the sinner's *incapacity* to see what stares him in the face (cf. what is said of the natural eyes in vs. 2 f., and of the eyes of the understanding in v. 4, which only God can open), and of his *defiance* of God's will (18 f.), for which he is wholly accountable.

The N.T. takes up the warning of v. 18 in Heb. **12**.15, where the familiar phrase a 'root of bitterness' needs the present context to clarify its meaning. What sounds there like a mere provocation to dissension or lowered standards is shown here to mean a prolific and stubborn source of apostasy. The phrase 'moist and dry alike' (19) is a characteristic mention of opposite extremes to denote a complete range of things, implying here that the judgement on such an apostasy would sweep away the whole nation, the innocent with the guilty. The threat of 'an overthrow like that of Sodom' (23) was all too nearly realized even in Isaiah's day (Isa. **1**.7–9), a full century before the Exile.

Verse 29 is one of the key statements of the scope and purpose of revelation, to be pondered for the limits it lays down, the assurances it offers, and the end it has in view. It should be the remembered motto of every theologian, preacher and student of the Word.

Deuteronomy 30 — 'With All Your Heart'

The promise of restoration (1–10). If the curses outweighed the blessings in ch. **28**, this passage shows grace superabundant where sin abounded. Note the 'when', not 'if', in v. 1; God knew what they would choose.

He knew also the shallowness of a repentance only born of hardship (cf. Hos. **6**.4; **7**.14); hence the necessity of the proviso repeated in vs. 2b,6b,10b, and of an inward work of grace to make it possible. The promise of v. 6 (complementing the command of **10**.16) is essentially that of the New Covenant which Jeremiah would prophesy in Jer. **31**.33. Those who point out, rightly enough, how little the covenant of Josiah's day touched the heart of Israel, must not blame Deuteronomy which prompted it; for no book of the O.T. emphasizes heart religion more.

The accessible Word (11–14). This memorable passage takes us gently to task for making a mystery of what God has made plain, just as the great statement of **29**.29 rebukes our hankering after what He has kept secret. Here is the true function of the law, as God's wisdom broken up small for man, for repetition and reflection (as in **6**.6 f.) which will issue in action (14). But this bringing of the word within man's reach was only a foretaste, as the N.T. shows. The pre-existent Word Himself would become flesh (John **1**.14), and Paul would be able to re-expound our passage in explicit terms of Christ, brought down from heaven and up from the dead (a realm even more inaccessible than 'beyond the sea'), and in terms of the gospel confessed and believed, to issue in salvation (Rom. **10**.5–10).

'*Therefore choose life*' (15–20). Once more, law and love are named in partnership (16), as in the teaching of the N.T. (e.g. John **14**.15; Rom. **13**.10). It is only when law is treated as the means of salvation that it is brought into conflict with the gospel (e.g Rom. 10.5–10, as above).

So 'life and good' (15) were man's to choose (19) but not to earn. The O.T. itself would bear witness to this and to salvation by grace through faith (e.g. Psa. 130; Psa. 143.2,7,8), just as the N.T. would call us to the good deeds that follow salvation (e.g. Rom. 8.4; Eph. 2.8–10). In our passage the unit is the nation, and the issues are stated in terms of its inheritance. But the equation in v. 20 is true for the one or the many: 'loving the Lord . . . means life'.

Deuteronomy 31 Changing Leadership, Unchanging Law

The transience of the most ageless of men is felt with some pathos in v. 2. So the paragraphs of this chapter alternate between the themes of proper change (1–8, 14 f., 23) and proper permanence. Moses' uplifting words to Israel and Joshua in vs. 3–8 were to remain in Joshua's memory and be divinely brought back to him on the eve of invasion (Josh. 1.6 ff.). How wholeheartedly Moses handed over to him can be judged from Num. 27.15 ff., where the appointment is shown as the answer to his own prayer (see comments there).

Verses 9–13,24–29. The periodic reading of the law, which used to be thought the fancy of a later age, accorded in fact with the conditions laid down in imperial treaties of the time of Moses, as did the depositing of this document in the sanctuary (cf. vs. 24–26). Note, too, the calling of 'heaven and earth to witness' (28), which corresponds, but in a very different form, to the clause which summoned various gods as witnesses to those agreements. (This feature persisted in the later treaties.)

So God turned familiar patterns to good account, bringing out the strongest features of the spoken and written word—the spoken having the direct appeal that a living voice can make to a great assembly, and the written having the accuracy that is needed for a binding agreement or constitution.

To all this, instructively enough, God added the special impact of song (19,21 f., 30), with its grip on the memory and its demand for expression ('it will live unforgotten in the mouths'—not at the back of the minds—'of their descendants' [21]). It is still one of the many good reasons for using song in worship and instruction, and for seeing that the song is striking and substantial.

5. OUR HOPE FOR YEARS TO COME: Deuteronomy 32—34

Deuteronomy 32 — The Song of Moses

This poem should be read with its object in mind: to be a standing witness to Israel of the sin and folly of apostasy, which God could see 'already forming' in His people's mind (31.21). So the past tenses of vs. 15–18,19–21, are 'prophetic perfects', referring chiefly to coming events which were already present to Him, although indeed Israel had turned to demons and false gods even in the wilderness (Exod. **32**.1; Lev. **17**.7; Num. **25**.2). Those who date the song later than Moses, to account for its allusions to an Israel corrupted by prosperity (15) and chastened by defeat (36), ignore this predictive, forewarning purpose (see especially **31**.20 f. for these very points.)

The pattern is as follows:

(i) *Introduction* (1–3). On the appeal to heaven and earth (1), see on **31**.28. Cf. **30**.19; Isa. **1**.2.

(ii) *Generous God, graceless people* (4–9). 'The Rock' (4) is a favourite term in this song (15,18,30 f., 37) and in many others, evocative of all that is enduring (Isa. **26**.4), towering (Psa. **61**.2) and protecting (Psa. **62**.2); yet it carries no suggestion of the impersonal—see vs. 6,18. 'Sons of Israel' is in the standard text of v. 8, but the Septuagint seems to have read 'Sons of *El*' (God) in the text it translated, and it is followed by the RSV. If this is right (it may not be), it contrasts the heathen, under the tutelage of principalities and powers (cf. Dan. **10**.13,20 f.), with Israel which enjoys the loving care of God Himself. In any case, the disputed meaning of v. 8 should not distract attention from its remarkable companion, v. 9 (strange treasure for God, then and now!).

(iii) *Loving nurture* (10–14) *and careless scorn* (15–18). In v. 10 'the apple of His eye' means 'the pupil . . .' In the beautiful picture of the eagle and its young (11), Moses employed one metaphor ('flutters . . .') which had portrayed God's Spirit creatively moving over the waters in Gen. **1**.2, and another ('bearing them . . .') which God had used in Exod. **19**.4 of transporting His people out of their enemies' reach to meet Him at His chosen place. 'Jeshurun' (15, cf. **33**.5,26; Isa. **44**.2) has the sound of an affectionate name based on the word 'right' (cf. 4b)—sadly ironical here. The demon-worship of v. 17 is seen in more terrible colours in Psa. **106**.37, and an unwelcome sequel to the 'new gods' is recorded in Judg. **5**.8.

(iv) *Provocation and counter-provocation* (19–27). How purposeful is God's harshness can be seen by comparing v. 21 with Rom.

10.19; **11**.11 ff.; and how restrained it is, from vs. 26 f.; cf. Ezek. **36**.23–28.

(v) *God and the no-gods* (28–42). The argument of the section is that although a final overthrow of Israel could only be the Lord's doing (30, cf. v. 26)—for the heathen gods are worse than useless (31–33)—the heathen themselves would misconstrue this (27–29). Therefore, the final reckoning will leave no room for doubt, and the reversal will be complete (34–42). Note the emphasis on divine retribution ('vengeance', 'recompense', 'requite'), which is taken up in Rom. **12**.19b. Note, too, in v. 39 the forerunner of the great monotheistic statements of Isa. **44**.8; **45**.5, etc. The song, as God intended (**31**.19), was the seed of some of the profoundest teachings of both Testaments.

(vi) *Doxology* (43). If this should be thought too fierce, see Luke **18**.7 f.; but it is judicial vengeance, not human spite (Luke **9**.54 f.; Rom. **12**.19).

The song delivered; the singer dismissed (44–52). Hard as this decree may seem, the fact remains that henceforth Moses' words were to be his greatest legacy, eclipsing even his deeds. It was the right moment to be called away.

Deuteronomy 33 — The Blessing of the Tribes

The companion to this chapter is Jacob's blessing of his sons in Gen. **49**. By definition, it looks ahead to their settlement in Canaan, and is therefore not to be dated by the conditions it predicts. (On the name Jeshurun [5], see on **32**.15.)

The prayer for *Reuben* (6) foresaw the danger of the tribe's decline and fall, exposed as it was to Moab, east of Jordan. But Judg. **5**.15 f. shows Reuben refusing the costly involvement with his fellow Israelites through which this prayer might have been answered.

Judah's blessing (7) should read as in the RV: '. . . with his hands he contended for himself; And [or But] thou shalt be a help . . .'—i.e. his danger, as a great tribe settled in the south, would be isolation and self-sufficiency. Largely through David, Judah's leading role in Israel as foretold in Gen. **49**.10 was indeed fulfilled. Incidentally, an echo of the missing Simeon's name may be intended in the opening word 'Hear' (cf. Gen. **29**.33, margin), for Simeon was destined to be merged with Judah. See on Num. **26**.14.

Levi (8–11) was perhaps tested and striven with (8) in the persons of Moses and Aaron, for whom Meribah was a fateful spot (**32**.51). The renouncing of family claims in v. 9 probably refers to the incident of Exod. **32**.29. It may also be a reminder of the total dedication still required of them—anticipating that of the Christian disciple. Note also the teaching duties of this tribe (10a); see references in the comment on Lev. **10**.11. For 'Thummim', etc. (8) see on Exod. **28**.30; Lev. **8**.8.

Commenting more briefly on the rest: the Temple was to lie just within *Benjamin's* border (and its courts apparently in Judah); hence the allusions to his favoured lot (12). 'His dwelling' may therefore mean 'God's dwelling' on Benjamin's hills, and the Christian can see his own privilege foreshadowed here (John **14**.23). *Joseph* (13–17), represented by *Ephraim* and *Manasseh* (17), was to occupy the 'choicest' part of the land: extensive, central and very fertile. Yet Hosea would have to say, 'All his riches can never offset the guilt he has incurred' (Hos. **12**.8).

Zebulun and *Issachar* (18 f.) were to live in the north, as were the remaining tribes of this chapter, except *Gad* (20 f.), which settled east of Jordan. In v. 19 the RSV has gratuitously inserted 'their', whereas the reference *may* be to the temple mount (Exod. **15**.17; Isa. **2**.3). In any case 'Galilee of the Gentiles' is called to bless the nations that enrich it (19); and we may remember that Zebulun was to include Nazareth (cf. Isa. **9**.1–7).

On the aggressive *Dan* (22), see Judg. **18**. *Naphtali's* 'lake' (23) was the Sea of Galilee. *Asher* ('Happy') (24) seems not to have lived up to its great possibilities. Did the refused challenge of Judg. **5**.17 become a habit?

The doxology (26–29) owes its magnificence partly to its exuberant vitality (e.g. 26,29b), but even more to its great range of vision, taking in height and depth, the fierce and the tender, blessings of peace and of war, defence and attack. God, to Moses, was no nebulous or neutral dignitary.

Deuteronomy 34 — The Death of Moses

The *narrative*, as elsewhere, speaks of Moses in the third person, and v. 10 implies that it was written a longish time after his death. But Moses' own words, the bulk of the book, were written by himself and carefully preserved (**31**.24–26). See also on Num. **12**.3.

Two traditional sites for v. 1, Jebel Neba and Jebel Osha, are discussed by G. T. Manley (*The Book of the Law*, pp. 63 f.), who writes of the second of these, 'The view from this peak corresponds so minutely with the description here given as to impress anyone who has been privileged to see it'. After an eyewitness account of the panorama, this author concludes, 'The description is as true as the view is marvellous'.

It is hard to resist a comparison between this mountain scene and that of the Temptation (Matt. 4.8). Here, the One who 'showed him all the land' (1) is the patient, scrupulous Lord whose best gifts are responsibilities not lightly granted (4) or lightly taken up (for Canaan was still an enemy stronghold), but are part of a design that is bigger than personal hopes and disappointments, and than death itself (see Luke 9.30). In the other scene the deceiver offers power and glory for a single gesture. But the glory is false, and the gesture would cost the One of whom it is asked all that He owes elsewhere, and all that He is. It was the same in Eden, and the pattern is still unaltered.

The book ends by looking forward as well as back, for the future was in good hands. 'The spirit of wisdom' which filled Joshua (9) is elsewhere indicated to be *the* Spirit (Num. 27.18). Even the note in vs. 10 ff. on the uniqueness of Moses as a prophet has its own content of hope, in view of the reiterated promise of 18.15,18, which was to live on in the expectation of Israel (John 1.21: Acts 3.22) until it was fulfilled beyond all imagining.

Questions for further study and discussion on Deuteronomy chs. 27—34

1. The curse of 27.26 must have seemed too sweeping to be seriously faced by most of its readers, for whom the curse of 21.23 was perhaps more of a talking-point after the crucifixion. Paul was enabled to wrestle with the truth of both curses. Follow his reasoning in Gal. 3 to its triumphant conclusion.
2. '. . . Till you are destroyed' (28.45). In view of v. 46, in what sense should we take this? Study the relation between God's covenant and His judgement in this chapter and in Hos. 1—3 and Rom 9—11.
3. With a reference Bible (RV references are the fullest) find out how much the Song of Moses (ch. 32) shaped the language and thought of later writers.
4. Compare the blessings of the tribes in ch. 33 with those of Gen. 49. What can we learn from this of the 'open-endedness' of God's promises and warnings (cf. Jer. 18.1–10)?